More than Laissez-Faire

More than Laissez-Faire

A Macroeconomic Textbook Alternative

*Divine Economy and Its Real World
Economic Principles*

BRUCE KOERBER

OL25683469M

To my wife Jeanne

and to my twin daughters,

Natalie and Leah.

Contents

Foreword

Most high school and college textbooks describe the nation's economy as a huge agglomeration of goods and services, vast piles of food, clothing, coal mines, factories, computers, agricultural products, kitchen appliances, TVs, automobiles, computers, planes, and so on ad infinitum. But these physical things are not the market economy as such. They are what people produce while working and trading in the market economy.

Bruce Koerber explains that the market economy is not a physical thing; rather it is a process, a human institution. It is at the same time the consequence of human actions and a shaper of human actors, transforming them into cooperative social human beings. The economy is the outgrowth of the purposive actions and choices of men. As such, it is manmade, but it is not purposively planned. As men meet, cooperate and have dealings with one another, markets evolve, as do societies and civilizations.

Koerber shows how the market economy develops. It is a dynamic process. Market participants are ego-driven; they act on the basis of their subjective values. Their subjective values are expressed in prices. Prices furnish knowledge about the wants and needs of other market participants. As traders turned from barter to using a medium of exchange, money, trading became easier. Moreover, money prices furnish market participants with information, knowledge, and the tools for calculation. Thus the market disseminates and coordinates the activities of market participants.

As Koerber explains, all men are driven by the human spirit to try to improve their situation. Individuals can best improve their respective situations when they are free to act. Therefore, the human spirit should be free. The right of individuals to private property must be protected so that individuals will save, accumulate capital and invest. If entrepreneurs are free to look for and to discover opportunities they tend to improve economic productivity. In the process, the free market economy develops economic principles and fosters law, order, justice and harmonious relations among all participants. Thus, the path to economic progress, peace, prosperity and a more advanced civilization is through the free market economy. On the other hand, when outside interventions interfere with the voluntary activities of individuals in the market economy, especially by wars and inflation, they violate property rights, disrupt the market's harmonious operations, distort prices and production, cause the boom/bust business cycles, and hamper economic progress.

For those who appreciate visual presentations of economic relationships, Koerber's book is sprinkled throughout with diagrams illustrating the influence on economic production of property rights, capital structure, prices, entrepreneurship, competition, profit and loss, etc.

Koerber's book explains that the free market economy is guided by voluntary actions. It is "in accord with the will of God." It leads to greater social cooperation, peace, increased prosperity and a more advanced civilization. It awakens the human spirit to its full potentiality. Koerber calls it the "divine economy."

Bettina Bien Greaves[1]
Hickory, North Carolina
February 2008

---

1. Formerly with the Foundation for Economic Education, Irvington-on-Hudson, NY; attended Mises' NYU graduate seminar on economic theory (1951–1969); compiled a 2-volume annotated bibliography of Mises' works, published by FEE in 1993 and 1995; and now editing the new editions of Mises' several works being published by Liberty Fund, Indianapolis, IN. The latest volume in their series is *Human Action* (2007).

List of Figures

Introduction:
Economic Vim And Verve

Imbibing Knowledge, New and Old

PREFACE

As we walked along the path that took us into the forest we came upon a clearing and in the middle of the clearing was a fire burning in a fire pit. Drawn to it we approached this 'life force' with heartfelt interest, pausing reflectively and feeling inspired; suddenly resolved to try to make sense out of this world of ours. It was this resolve, this new quest, that was exceptional and it exhibited in us a strong sense of vitality.

Apparently we must have imbibed a spirit of enthusiasm from exposure to this 'life force' energy. With conviction we now determinedly realize that it is time to explore reality further. Filled with enthusiasm, and combining it with knowledge and wisdom, we take it upon ourselves to transform our quest into a journey. It is along this journey where new ideas are expressed and encapsulated into theory.

THE DISCOVERY

Our journey is a journey of discovery. What is remarkable is that without even taking a step we discover wonders that are awesome. The economy is everywhere. It is all around us and it is in us. Its pervasiveness is remarkable.

Additionally we find great potency and exuberant vitality at each point where the economy becomes manifest. To act is to bring into existence something new which coalesces with everything else that already exists. This powerful force is part of human life.

And yet few of us realize what is at our fingertips. With what enthusiasm should we embrace this inherent power that is our birthright?
If we can get past being overwhelmed by such a thought then we can
truly begin to appreciate this creative force. It is the mirror image of the
creative force that brings together the letter B and the letter E to form
the word 'BE' and it is!

THE CYCLE

The journey is part of our evolution and it is part of our maturity. What
we discover during the journey is both the old and the new. From our
vantage point it is the past that gives us footing, and it is the new reaches
we make that take us towards the summit. But this perspective—the
recognition that we are at a vantage point—is a sign of the times. We
are at a special point in the cycle of human affairs.

The fact that the divine economy theory is now discovered is
evidence that we are in a new cycle. At the same time this new cycle
has a nature about it that requires a new theory. Reciprocally then,
the discovery of the divine economy theory and the need for the divine
economy theory are both important in this cycle, in this particular era
of human history.

Chapter 1
Divine Economy Theory

Its Germination

PREFACE

Encapsulated within the shell of the seed coat is the theory of economics. It has set there for ages and is in direct contact with the earth and the earthly conditions. Those seeds that were not viable succumbed to the oxidizing forces of the earth. Among the viable seeds there were two kinds remaining: the weeds, and the true seeds of economic science. We want to discard the weed seeds and we want to understand the organism of true economic science, as set forth in the divine economy theory.

ACTIVATION

We will start by asking the question: What would it take to bring together the theory and the reality of the economy? The answer lies in a process similar to germination, a process which has been activated by the great forces at play in the world right now. Knowledge in the garb of newness perceptibly exists. It attracts our attention because we are remarkably entrepreneurial in spirit. At that instant a new germ begins to grow and the vital process within it has an inherent nature that transforms itself and its surroundings. Then this new and transformed knowledge of reality finds its way into theory, hence there is a union here between theory and reality.

How can our current plight and the past plight of humanity be reconciled with the human potential for good? Of course no one thinks that humans are perfect. Errors and mistakes are clear signs of imperfection. However, relative perfection is possible and this degree of perfection occurs most readily when the flow of information is optimal. In our search for perfection each of us is attracted to those things that bring about human prosperity, which in essence is the equivalent of the 'expression of oneself.'

New insight into the economy will come shortly—as it is presented in this book—and these insights will reveal new possibilities. What has to be assumed so far from these introductory remarks is that what has germinated is a mighty apple tree that will grow stronger and stronger. And its branches will provide a sheltering canopy. The further along in its developmental stages the more it alters its own surroundings which then becomes a key feature in and of itself. As it matures its vitality becomes increasingly evident and significant.

ECONOMICS TO THE CORE

The origin of the economy is intricately intertwined with the origin of man, which is ancient and even still a mystery. It taxes all the discerning powers of historians and archeologists to discover the origin of man. Why does this veiled past have anything to do with the economy? The premise of this book is that the economy is a uniquely human institution and that without the human being there would be no such thing as the economy. Speaking in these terms it is obvious that they both appear and evolve concurrently.

The intimately woven fabric composed of both humanity and of the economy necessitates a deep examination into the nature of mankind. What we find is that the human urge to act is irresistible, and that human action stems from the same source as human reason.

Although rudimentary in the early stages of development, the early actions taken by primitive human beings were very much of the moment and yet they were also important agents of transformation. Notice the dynamic here—the spontaneity between the act and the transformation—a dynamic that conveys great meaning. One does not exist without the other and yet each spark of interplay reveals new possibilities. It is then this cumulative effect of human actions and the subsequent transformation, taken throughout time and across time, which brings to us the modern economy.

A moment of reflection is now needed for us to be able to discern what is real and foundational. As I just mentioned, the economy is a uniquely human institution. Since the human being can dwell in the world of relative perfection or imperfection the potential then exists for the economy to be in one of two states. If the higher nature of humanity is realized then the institution (the economy) that is a tool for the expression of human action will itself be elevated and celestial. Frankly, it is the divine nature of the human being which is his true reality and therefore it can be deduced that the highest potential of the institution of the economy is divine.

What is the current condition of the modern economy? It is true that the modern economy carries the cumulative effect of human actions taken over time. Errors from economic ignorance have accumulated, consequently along the way unnecessary burdens have been added. These add weight and bulk, since after all, the burdens are cumulative.

The metaphorical divine charger, because of these cumulative burdens, cannot traverse the span of contemporary history nimbly and ably. It may stumble. It may have to reverse or change courses. These burdens slow the arrival of the triumph of prosperity, which is our birthright provided we recognize and endeavor to attain our divine nature.

We must sort out the reason for the burdening or weakening of the institution (the economy) that serves to bring about our betterment. Understanding human nature sheds some light on the subject. The will to choose the higher perfections versus choosing the imperfections of our lower nature is at the crux. It turns out that ego-driven intervention is the best economic example of humans exercising their lower nature. Just as metal oxidizes and becomes corrupt, so too the economy deteriorates when it is corrupted by intervention.

The Nature of the Economy

Herein lays the beginning of the problem that needs to be dealt with using economic science. The economy which is viewed as a human institution, has not been seen up until now and as I propose, as divine. The economy has a pure form to be striven towards.

How do we know what the uncorrupt economy looks like unless it is seen as having a pure form? Those who recognize that the economy operates perfectly well independently hold "laissez-faire" up as the pure form. But they have not made any connection to the divine nature of the human being as an essential identity. This is a new thought and is worthy of consideration.

Granting that the economy is divine implies the following: that the actors are seen as expressive agents of the will of mankind, that there is no omniscience within the realm of human policy-making that can even minutely compare to the divine expression inherent in the market, and that the market is not a product of human design. The market is a divine institution that emerges spontaneously from human action. It is a social institution that forms for the sake of production. The market is the time and place where the convergence of all of this useful information transpires and where it is discovered.

THE MARKET PROCESS

Every exchange takes place in a market which makes clear the point that the word 'market' is most certainly universal and almost infinitely broad. As stated with eloquence by Mises:

> Choosing determines all human decisions. In making his choice man chooses not only between various material things and services. All human values are offered for option. All ends and all means, both material and ideal issues, the sublime and the base, the noble and the ignoble, are ranged in a single row and subjected to a decision which picks out one thing and sets aside another. Nothing that men aim at or want to avoid remains outside of this arrangement into a unique scale of gradation and preference. The modern theory of value widens the scientific horizon and enlarges the field of economic studies.[11, p. 3]

It is clear then that subjective values are within the realm of economics. When an exchange does occur it is based on the knowledge-at-hand by the actors—the buyer and the seller. The knowledge-at-hand is relative and imperfect, yet at the same time it is fully coordinated within time and space. In other words, it could not be made more perfect as evidenced by the willingness of both the buyer and the seller to consummate the exchange, free of any coercion to do so.

There are those who object to the imperfect knowledge of the actors, insisting that they would have made a better decision if they had perfect knowledge. This objection is certainly naïve and contrary to the real world. Human beings are neither omniscient nor omnipresent. They cannot grasp all that came before nor do they know the future with certainty. All actors in the economy have only partial knowledge.

The "single mind" that has all knowledge does find expression in this new concept of a divine economy. It happens through the instrument (the market) nestled within the divine institution (the economy) bestowed upon mankind. In other words, the unique instrument of human expression that forms as the foundation of economics is the market.

Human planners of the economy are hopeless failures and can be more aptly described as oppressors. In the real economy (the divine economy) there is a 'central planner' who is all-knowing and all-seeing and perfectly just. It is God.

God is the creator of the economy as a human institution and His design allows the fullest expression of human diversity. In the divine economy there is decentralized planning to the nth degree, where n represents each individual or business entity that is actively interacting within the market process. The economy changes as the human race changes and yields its promised fruits conditionally—depending upon whether the current state of affairs exists as either a hampered or an unhampered market.

The state of affairs at any point in time reflects the spiritual maturity of mankind and the corresponding condition of the economy. As mankind, as a whole, matures he increasingly cares for himself and for others. The economy always fully serves at the level it is capable of as an institution with divine potential, but unfortunately it has historically been significantly constrained by human intervention.

Like all institutions the economy has the appearance of structure. Its structure in its pure form is the market, free from political intervention. The closer the economy is to a free market the greater its capacity to be a full expression of a divine economy.

Remember that there is interplay between the human actors and the market itself. There is a commingling of these two divine entities and both benefit from this dynamic process of discovery. Also there is a transforming power in this divine encounter.

This transforming power is perhaps the most essential element of the divine economy. There is a divine power—the power to transform the resources bestowed upon us into goods and services and which then enables us to serve one another as a tribute to our loving Creator.

More Than Meets the Eye

The divine economy has the power to awaken us to our own potential, which finds expression in service to one another and to our loving Creator. That is why the progress of humanity, even for us as individuals, depends on a free market. Likewise, the discovery of the merits of the divine economy depends on the educative process—significantly derived from the market experience itself—from which proceeds the ever-advancing progress of humanity.

The critical need is to bring all of these processes of the divine economy into the realm of science. Here the groundwork has already been laid by the great minds who have described the methodology of subjectivism and who have expounded upon praxeology—which is the study and logic of human action. This great scientific heritage pays tribute to monumental thinkers such as Thomas Aquinas, Carl Menger, Eugene von Böhm-Bawerk, Ludwig von Mises, Friedrich von Hayek, and Murray Rothbard. From their work and the work that continues along these lines there is a scientific foundation that provides the tools needed to test and to advance the understanding of the processes at work.

Since human beings act purposefully the power to make the divine economy manifest rests with each individual. It rests; it resides, and becomes evident in these individual actions. Mises writes:

> As long as a man lives, he cannot help obeying the cardinal impulse, the *élan vital*. It is man's innate nature that he seeks to preserve and to strengthen his life, that he is discontented and aims at removing uneasiness, that he is in search of what may be called happiness.[11, p. 882]

The power to make the divine economy manifest comes from the invisible world of thought and reason and enters the visible world through purposeful action. Since no action occurs in a vacuum each action becomes a part of the educative matrix of all actions, all of which follow the same subjective processes.

What is incredible is how the subjectivist methodology of classical liberalism allows the merging of science and religion. This subjectivist methodology can be used to discern the essential laws that apply universally to human beings when they are at the threshold of action, whether that act is an act of faith or a material act. These universal laws ultimately underlie our quest to know and to understand.

We are educated and we make advancements by the insights gained during our quest for understanding. In the realm of faith our souls progress and our nature becomes more divine. In the material realm we become more tuned in to how our interconnectedness with others can bring prosperity and how we benefit personally from that prosperity.

It is not something that we may even have to consciously make decisions about. It becomes, in a sense, just a realization. This parallels a statement attributed to the British mathematician and metaphysician Alfred North Whitehead, as quoted by Hayek, "Civilization advances by extending the number of important operations which we can perform without thinking about them."[3, p. 528]

The divine economy is not separable from human civilization, nor is it separable from the advancement of human culture at the individual or societal level. The divine economy operates in accordance with the Will of God and it is a vehicle for the expression of the will of man. The implication of the divine economy is that there are laws and that there is order.

The power within and without the divine economy is beyond our grasp. Yet throughout history men have sought to grasp it. Examples throughout history abound. For the short while and ephemeral period that the power-hungry clutched the economy their illusion of control corrupted them, and the economy became distorted and diverted, leading to the suffering of many both near and distant. Ultimately the destiny of mankind was slowed by their intervention. Quoting Rothbard:

> "The hidden order, harmony and efficiency of the voluntary free market, the hidden disorder, conflict and gross inefficiency of coercion and intervention—these are the great truths that economic science, through deductive analysis of self-evident axioms, reveals to us."[8, p. 1124]

There is only One Being omniscient enough to see all that happens in the market matrix and only One Being that is not wholly dumbfounded by what human minds see as uncertainty. The economy is divine, it is God's.

The economy provides channels through which the grace and bounty of God flow. According to the divine economy theory, the economy (itself a divine institution) is reciprocally a part of the human operating system. The sooner we learn this and trust this the sooner we can learn how to use this institution to bring about peace and justice.

The divine economy is here for our benefit. It forces us (acting man) non-coercively and by the tendencies of the forces of equilibrium to refine ourselves internally (heart and soul, spirit and intellect), and externally (human and non-human resources). And so it is that the equilibrium forces referred to in this book as the 'divine economy' direct our refinement.

Chapter 2
Divine Economy Model ©

Organic and subjective and splendid!

PREFACE

Our journey has now brought us face-to-face with another 'life force.' Unlike the fire encountered in the forest, this 'life force' is organic and subjective. Yet it is similar to the fire since it, too, is splendid. It is organic because of its symmetry and reciprocity and because it manifests characteristics of life. Its life-likeness is directly attributable to its DNA and its RNA; that is, to its foundation and its operation, which rest upon subjectivism. From this subjective nature we see what can fittingly be described as dynamic splendor.

THE CODE

Shortly I will begin to present to you a graphical representation of the divine economy model. But before we begin examining the model we will want to understand the conceptual basis of what is called the Cartesian coordinate system. In mathematics the applications of the two dimensional coordinate system and of the three dimensional coordinate system appear to be very empirical. Despite being used mostly for empirical work the Cartesian coordinate system is not restricted from more conceptual applications, as proven when it is expanded to higher dimensions, for example, the fourth dimension, the fifth dimension or even to the nth 'degrees of freedom.'

I take advantage of the conceptual potentialities of the Cartesian coordinate system and use it as a part of the design of my subjective model. Just as the higher dimensions are abstract I make all of the dimensions of my model abstract. Referring to the Cartesian coordinate system, Bernhard Riemann in 1854 described the value of this abstraction: "Abstract studies such as these allow one to observe relationships without being limited by narrow terms, and prevent traditional prejudices from inhibiting ones progress." In my model the two dimensional system is subjective or 'abstract' as is the third dimension and the fourth dimension and the fifth dimension, in other words, my model is five dimensional.

The Conceptual Model

Now I will introduce the divine economy model to you. As the model is presented; its interconnectedness, reciprocity and symmetry will be discussed. One analogy that may prove useful is that of a complex organism made up of components that are more or less differentiated. Ourselves, we are made up of systems and organs and tissues and cells. Likewise the divine economy model has universal laws, foundational elements, concepts, and principles.

The center of the model is its reality and essence, summed up using the words 'divine economy.' These two powerful words clearly state the vital perspective of this model. These two words efficiently convey the source and the dominion. The implication here is far more magnificent than laissez-faire which merely suggests 'not to meddle.' The implication here is that the economy is above and beyond our human understanding and that it can be and is corrupted by human intervention alone.

The divine economy is both pervasive and subtle and its dominion reaches everyone in their daily affairs. It is basic and connected to the necessary acts of every man and woman and by its conveyance of information it allows people to function.

The Two Dimensional Model

Just as there are four cardinal directions; a north and south and east and west, the organic divine economy model has four petals. Gleaned from the knowledge and insight of many great thinkers I chose the following petals for the model: human spirit, transformation, law, and order. What we have is the model in its simplest form (see Diagram 2a).

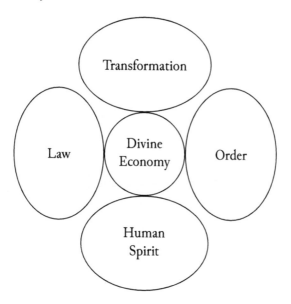

Diagram 2a: Anatomy of the divine economy

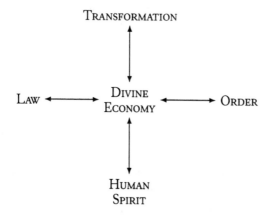

Diagram 2b: Skeletal structure of the divine economy

To the model we then add reciprocity and symmetry (Diagram 2b). From now on you will notice arrows on both ends of the lines to represent reciprocity and symmetry. The element of reciprocity adds the dimension of mutual exchange. Another way to describe what happens during an exchange is to see exchange as the fulfillment of the double inequality of wants. I want what you have more than what I have and you reciprocate those feelings, therefore we exchange.

Proportionality and relativity manifest themselves in the world via the element of symmetry. For example, as transformation within the economy increases the other vital elements of the economy also increase and the economy as a whole increases. The model now becomes what is seen in Diagram 2b.

In this form the functionality of the model begins to emerge. It has a dynamic nature. Every point is relative to every other point and every understanding gained causes movement, advancing civilization.

To continue to improve the functionality of the model more scientific elements of the economy are added. These economic elements were discovered by great thinkers in the tradition of classical liberalism. These certain points of focus are added to the skeletal structure as intermediary potencies.

To the skeleton we add more substance making the model more realistic and bringing it to life. To the human spirit appendage we add action, purposeful action. To the transformation appendage we add capital structure. The law appendage fills out nicely with property rights and it is the market that beefs up the order appendage.

With this added substance, as shown in Diagram 2c, it begins to become evident to us how the model neatly incorporates the intermediary elements that make it operational. Using the analogies of a skeletal structure and appendages reminds us about the organic nature of the model.

This is the highest form of the two dimensional model and this is where the model begins to become complex. We will have to take a step back and examine more deeply the foundational components. Then the extremely potent intermediary elements will need to be explored.

Going back to the skeletal structure of the divine economy in Diagram 2b it is easy to see how interactive and cumulatively interactive it is. The human being has a nature that is subject to illumination. It is the human spirit that reflects that reality. Transformation is the illumination that takes place and this all comes about because we encounter the human spirit of others, directly or indirectly. The world is not a vacuum, people learn from others and from their environment.

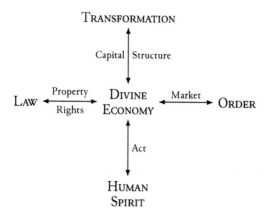

Diagram 2c: Modus operandi of the divine economy

The world has structure and incorporating structure into our lives creates order. Transformation is furthered by discovering the operational laws of that order. Completing the circle, then, the human spirit is illumined by the transformation that has taken place.

The dynamic interaction of all of these interrelated elements is certain. Already it is clear that the complexity of the divine economy is mind boggling. We have to trust in its divine nature and content ourselves with understanding bits and pieces, ever humbled by the infinite greatness of the divine economy.

Now moving on to the more complex model in Diagram 2c—the modus operandi of the divine economy—we need to spend some time educating and re-educating ourselves about these intermediary elements. It would be inaccurate and naïve to pretend that there is a common understanding of these four elements in the economic literature or in the minds of most readers.

The four scientific elements that make up the modus operandi of the divine economy are property rights, human action, the market, and capital structure. These are potent forces which universally permeate human life on this planet!

Placement of these intermediate elements into the model relative to the initial foundational components expands the foundation of the model. The model readily accommodates the fluid manner in which these eight elements all juxtapose themselves.

Property rights interface closely with human action, the market and the capital structure. Property rights are truly foundational and have a strong connection to law in the divine economy since they anchor the economy to the human being. In its most basic and primary expression, property rights are human rights. The existence of a human being grants dominion, and its peaceful expansion toward food, clothing and higher attainments all fall within the domain of property rights.

The human spirit—each one of us as a unique expression of the grace of God—becomes foundational in the divine economy through human action. Human action is the expression of the human spirit, which implies that the human spirit is the locus of communication and serves as a channel for the two-way flow of knowledge.

Understanding that the economy is a uniquely human institution means there is also cognition that the human spirit is where it all begins and human action is where it becomes manifest. Without human beings, whose nature it is to act purposefully, there would be no economy.

There is a saying: 'It takes two to tango!' That is what the market is. It is the place where the solitary individual becomes a social being.

By this very broad definition the interaction of parents with their children could even be considered a market. Although an argument could be forwarded against this line of reasoning such an argument does not allow this very important point to be made therefore it serves no purpose here. The purpose of this broad definition is to remove the limiting definitions ascribed to the market and to remove the prejudices about the market.

The market is where individual human action undergoes reconfiguration into a more social entity. This is part of the dynamics between the 'act' and the 'transformation.' The market is where knowledge flows to and from in a civilization. And it is from this proverbial fountain of knowledge that order emerges. See Diagram 2d.

The three scientific elements just described—property rights, human action, and the market—are inherent and found in full potential in the divine economy. The fourth element differs slightly from the others because of its very strong ties to time.

The fourth element, capital structure, is also foundational. It contains and conveys the knowledge that all things in this world are subject

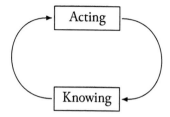

Diagram 2d: Proverbial fountain: part of the transformation process

to the law of time. Capital, the means of stretching production beyond the present, is necessarily foundational also.

Most significantly, of all factors in the economy capital is the most limiting. See if you understand why. Ponder: in the here and now—in the present—we cannot live in the future! That is our limitation. The reason capital is the most limiting is because it is what connects the present and the future in the economy within 'our limitation.' It is constrained by uncertainty yet its variation or structure determines the transformation that takes place in the economy.

Since capital is the most limiting factor, the movement or advancement of civilization depends heavily upon the structure of capital. This necessitates, optimally, that the capital structure needs to be a harmonious expression of the market so that it truthfully reflects the will of the people. In the divine economy fully vested human beings find and share knowledge in the market. Part of that knowledge reflects the importance of time which becomes manifest in capital and its relevant structure.

THE THREE DIMENSIONAL MODEL

The next modification of the divine economy model stretches the imagination a little by adding a depth dimension, the third dimension in this model. This can be grasped fairly easily by imagining the modus operandi of the divine economy given in Diagram 2c as submerged in a bowl of water. The water that surrounds and supports the model represents latent and active entrepreneurship. See Diagram 2e.

Entrepreneurship is alertness to one's surroundings and the knowledge therein. This is nearly perfectly represented by the 'submersion' analogy. The water is what surrounds ('one's surroundings') and submersion into the water introduces entrepreneurship. In this

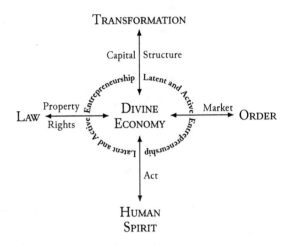

Diagram 2e: The driving force of the divine economy

entrepreneurial condition all that is within ('the knowledge therein') potentially comes to light.

When entrepreneurship is in the latent state the divine economy and its components are in potential only. When alertness triggers a response the result is active entrepreneurship, which significantly, is the driving force in the economy.

If I am in a latent state of entrepreneurship I may simply buy a product that I like. Or I may begin to actively perceive opportunities and compare and contrast to see what other products are out there to buy or sell. Additionally I may look at the time horizon. I may weigh the various possibilities and decide to save so that I can buy a tractor because of the prospect of improved production, for example.

As an active entrepreneur I may discover discrepancies in the market that lead to inefficiencies and I may take steps to remedy the situation. When in a latent state, the water merely holds within it the divine economy. But when there is active entrepreneurship, energy is released which charges all of the elements in the water.

The Fourth Dimension

The fourth dimension of the divine economy model enters into the picture by identifying its poles. The divine economy has many components just like the complex system of the planet Earth which has numerous components such as the water cycle, the ocean currents, the atmospheric forces, geothermal forces, and absorption of solar radiation to name a few. The Earth also can be understood more fully by examining these factors as they are influenced by rotation around its poles.

Similarly the divine economy can be more fully understood when the model includes the poles of unity and justice (Diagram 2f). It is around these two poles that the divine economy revolves. The axis of these poles represents the 'nature and role of knowledge.' The implication here—with this axis being centrally located within the model—is that knowledge flows throughout and that it is this free-flowing knowledge that best serves all of the divine economy processes.

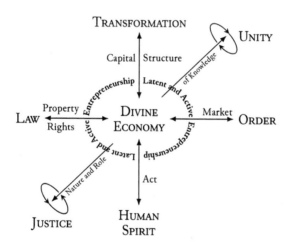

Diagram 2f: The complete Divine Economy Model independent of time

This is a key concept in the divine economy theory. It is the nature and role of knowledge that enables the equilibrium forces to maintain balance and harmony. Intervention by those with finite human understanding strikes at the 'nature and role of knowledge' axis—with the consequences being a condition of imbalance and disharmony and a corruption of the divine economy.

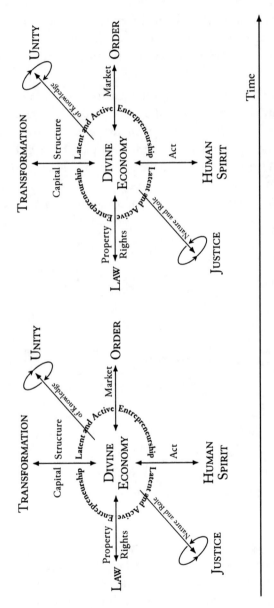

Diagram 2g: The complete Divine Economy Model over time

To clarify the importance of justice, it is justice that inextricably links the interests of the individual and those of society. Justice also implies non-violence and non-coercion.

Elaborating on the pole of unity; the pole of unity shines with prosperity for all. There is now an awareness of the historical and scientific knowledge that shows all of humanity as one people. As far back as A.D. 1573 Bartolome de Albornoz wrote:

> Buying and selling is the nerve of human life that sustains the universe. By means of buying and selling the world is united, joining distant lands and nations, people of different languages, laws and ways of life. [1, Ch. 7, 29]

THE FIFTH DIMENSION

The fifth dimension of the divine economy model brings in the realism of time since there is no realism to any economic model that is static. The dynamicism of all of the elements of the model comes to life as changes take place over time (Diagram 2g).

Now that the complete model of the divine economy is defined we are ready to examine economic production. The Divine Economy Model© is conducive to the graphical and conceptual exploration of production possibilities frontiers, as you will find out in the next chapter.

Selected Exercises

1. What is it that convinces you that the Divine Economy Model© is a subjective model?

2. Explain how all of the elements in the Divine Economy Model© are affected by the equilibrium forces.

Chapter 3
Production Possibilities Frontiers

The Branches of the Divine Economy Model©

PREFACE

The structure of this organic and subjective organism is strong and its framework can withstand the test of time and the tests that come from outside forces. Growth is a main feature and a natural part of the process. Some conditions enhance and some conditions hinder this process. As stewards it is our responsibility to understand what causes growth so we can create a healthy environment for the economy.

A MACROECONOMIC TOOL

Now that the complete model of the divine economy is defined (Diagrams 2f and 2g) we can examine production. Production constraints, in general, are defined by laws such as property rights, by the order given within the market, by transformation that is molded within the capital structure, and by the human spirit which is entrepreneurial by nature and expressed as human action.

To begin we will start with the production possibilities frontier that is the most familiar. By familiar I do not mean readily understood but rather I mean that it is the one production possibilities frontier that has been examined most thoroughly in the economic literature. For example in *Time and Money: The Macroeconomics of Capital Structure*[2, pp. 40–45] Roger Garrison uses the standard production possibilities frontier (PPF) technique to illustrate the trade-offs between capital goods and consumption goods. See Diagram 3a.

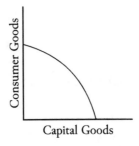

Diagram 3a: The standard production possibilities frontier (PPF)

As you can see it is an 'either/or' proposition. More of one 'good' comes at the expense of the other. In other words, to have more capital goods it is necessary to sacrifice some consumer goods. The underlying cause is that both have at least some of the same inputs meaning that the output of one channels the inputs away from the other. When we examine Diagram 3a it becomes obvious that the frontier is defined by two axes and these axes are two opposing aggregates. The relative position along the frontier is a net output. Since these are aggregates we are talking about macroeconomics.

It's now time to see how the production possibilities frontier diagram works. At some point on the frontier the output gain over time from a certain mix of 'inputs' is equal to the output loss from channeling 'inputs' in the alternative direction. This condition represents a stationary economy, for example, consider an economy where gross investment is offset exactly by capital depreciation. Considering that capital is the most limiting factor in the economy, the consequence is a no-growth economy. See Diagram 3b.

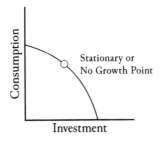

Diagram 3b: Stationary or no growth economy

This point can be viewed as a conceptual ratio of one output to the other. In our example the economy is stationary and at the 'no growth point' when consumption (C) = investment (I) in a symbolical sense, written in a shorthand form as the ratio of $C/I = 1$.

Let us now consider the two other economic conditions. If $C > I$ the point on the frontier lies north and west of the 'no growth' point. As such capital depreciation exceeds capital investment which weakens the economy. The cascading effect of this condition is economic contraction. Notice the inward movement over time in Diagram 3c.

> Since capital structure is an essential part of the transformation process, capital is the most limiting factor in the economy.

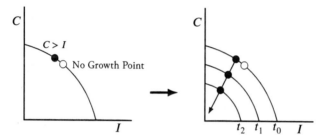

Diagram 3c: Economic contraction

Conversely if $C < I$ the point on the frontier curve lies south and east of the 'no growth' point. See Diagram 3d. Since capital is the most limiting factor in the economy the cascading effect of investment being greater than consumption is an expanding economy over time.

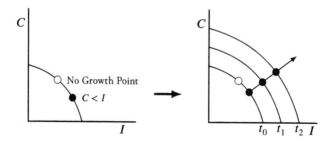

Diagram 3d: Economic expansion

Now the task becomes one of translating the production possibilities frontier into the language of the divine economy theory. Our
starting point is the foundational component referred to in the Divine
Economy Model© as 'Transformation.' The basic economic element
of 'Transformation' is the capital structure which is also referred to as
an intermediary potency. As you can see, not coincidentally, we are
now able to connect the divine economy theory directly to the standard
production possibilities frontier, and subsequently to contemporary
economic literature, via the relationship of consumer goods to capital
goods—the capital structure.

Transformation Element of the Divine Economy Model

This first link is sufficient to begin translating the rest of the foundational components of the Divine Economy Model© into the production
possibilities frontier format for further analysis. In this first link shown in
Diagram 3e (comparable to Diagram 3a) we start with 'Transformation'
and we find that its production possibilities frontier is like a snapshot
taken of the capital structure. Since this 'Transformation' PPF is identical
to the 'standard production possibilities frontier' all that remains to be
done is to select which divine economy component to examine next.

Diagram 3e: 'Transformation' production possibilities frontier

So next we will take a look at the most foundational of all of
the components of the Divine Economy Model© and that is 'Human
Spirit.' The economy exists only because humans exist and because they
act as humans do. See Diagram 3f.

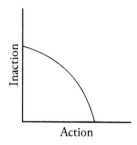

Diagram 3f: 'Human Spirit' production possibilities frontier

HUMAN SPIRIT ELEMENT OF THE DIVINE ECONOMY MODEL

The unique and challenging opportunity afforded us is to further define this frontier by identifying the equivalent point that represents a stationary or 'no growth' economy since such a point exists for all production possibilities frontiers. See Diagram 3g.

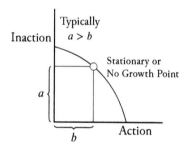

Diagram 3g: 'Human Spirit' no growth point

This 'no growth' point can be viewed as naturally occurring and as part of the response of humans to uncertainty and imperfect knowledge. The paralysis of growth at the 'no growth' point can be understood conceptually as Action = Inaction, in aggregate!

What a strange statement! What it means is that relative to a free market (or an unhampered economy) the inaction is great, so great that actions cannot offset the lost opportunities. For example, intervention increases the degree of imperfect knowledge in the market causing opportunities to be lost.

In contrast, however, if the point on the frontier lies south and east of the 'no growth' point, action prevails, which means the human spirit is being fulfilled. See Diagram 3h.

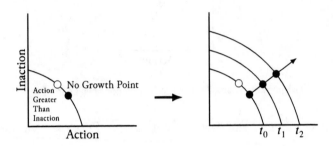

Diagram 3h: 'Human Spirit' expanding economy

When the point lies north and west of the 'no growth' point on the frontier inaction is greater than action which moves the human spirit in the direction of inertia, which is where the human spirit begins to resemble lower forms such as the animal or even a vegetative state. In other words, entrepreneurship is stifled. What could dampen the human spirit like that? The answer: Anything that creates veils so that uncertainty increases and imperfect knowledge becomes more pervasive and daunting. See Diagram 3i.

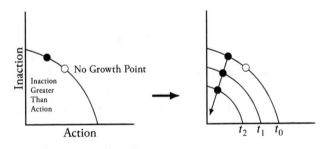

Diagram 3i: 'Human Spirit' contracting economy

The next production possibilities frontier illustrates how the potency of the third foundational component of the Divine Economy Model © 'Law'—whether it is natural law or divine law or man-made law—constrains production.

Law Element of the Divine Economy Model

As it pertains to us humans the most basic of all rights is the human right and in the divine economy theory we have the following core identity: human rights = property rights, and its mirror image: property rights = human rights. The point on the production possibilities frontier that represents the stationary economy is where encumbrances exactly offset freedom. See Diagram 3j.

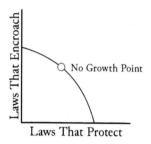

Diagram 3j: 'Law' production possibilities frontier and the no growth point

    This production possibilities frontier is useful when contemplating the concept of liberty. If the point on the frontier lies south and east of the 'no growth' point then property rights are increasing and so are human rights and liberty. In an environment such as this the economy expands and people feel prosperous. See Diagram 3k.

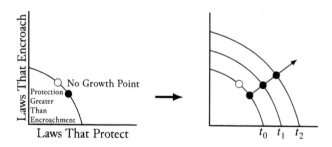

Diagram 3k: 'Law' expanding economy

    In contrast, when the point lies north and west of the 'no growth' point on the frontier laws that encroach upon liberties cause their baleful effects on the economy leading to a contraction. As property rights are whittled away, for instance, the production possibilities frontiers shrink, as shown in Diagram 3l.

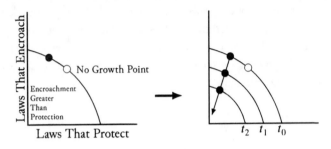

Diagram 3l: 'Law' contracting economy

The final foundational element of the Divine Economy Model© is 'Order.' Consider the different outcomes resulting from a system that has order and a system that is in chaos. It is in this sense that 'Order' affects production as portrayed by the following production possibilities frontier.

ORDER ELEMENT OF THE DIVINE ECONOMY MODEL

What is meant by spontaneous order is the unhampered market guided by voluntary actions. The 'no growth' point on the frontier has some-times been referred to as a 'mixed economy' where the gains from knowledge flowing in the market are offset by losses that come from arbitrary and erroneous data caused by intervention in the economy. See Diagram 3m. For example, prices that are manipulated when the money supply is artificially altered send misleading signals through-out the market causing at the same time both over-consumption and malinvestment.

One of the great outcomes of the divine economy theory will be an economically literate humanity. Basic to such an understanding is the justice, the ethics, and the optimality of the spontaneous order of the market. A point lying south and east of the 'no growth' point is an example of movement in that direction and the result is an expanding economy. See Diagram 3n.

All interventionists, no matter how well intended, fall significantly short of comprehending the infinitely dynamic economy. Consequently

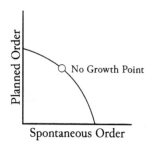

Diagram 3m: 'Order' production possibilities frontier

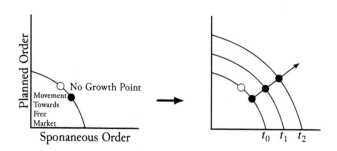

Diagram 3n: 'Order' expanding economy

all planning of the economy moves the point north and west along the production possibility frontier. The long run effects of all planning and intervention, despite the politically motivated short run results, cause a contraction of the economy. See Diagram 3o.

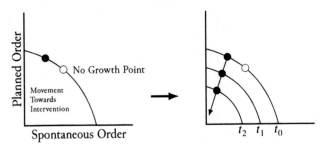

Diagram 3o: 'Order' contracting economy

I will conclude this chapter with a final thought. When conditions are right for an expanding economy the effect is universal. Similarly the effects of a contracting economy are also universal, however, the equilibrium force that is inherent in the economy naturally eliminates the deleterious effects of interventionism once the intervention is stopped at its source. It is cast ashore like the foam on the ocean and discarded as worthless. In contrast, the equilibrium force operating in the expanding economy nurtures in ways described in the divine economy theory, and that leads naturally to an ever-advancing civilization. See Diagram 3p.

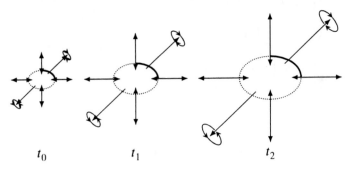

Diagram 3p: Divine economy sphere frontiers of an ever-advancing civilization

This is a good point in the book to bring to your attention the conceptual connection between the production possibilities frontier and the divine economy sphere frontiers shown in Diagram 3p. Production possibilities frontiers are simply two-dimensional quadrant diagrams. Notice in Diagram 3p the enlarging sphere for entrepreneurial discovery. Relative to the production possibilities frontier of the earlier economy (as it moves from t_0 to t_1 to t_2) there is more spontaneous order (market) and there is more law (liberty). Relative to the earlier economy the potential of transformation is greater and the capacity and potential of the human spirit is increased. Justice and unity are relatively more advanced due to the evolution of the nature and role of knowledge. These are the divine economy sphere frontiers that are a part of the divine economy theory.

And guess what, there is no reason why the relative changes of all of these potentialities cannot continue endlessly. The divine economy releases all of these energies, generation after generation. This is now a proven fact according to and given by the divine economy theory.

Selected Exercises

1. Describe the meaning of the frontiers (t_0, t_1, and t_2) in the standard production possibilities frontier and also in the divine economy frontiers (as shown in Diagram 3p) in terms of limited resources.

2. Contrast the difference between planned order and spontaneous order.

Chapter 4
Real World Economic Principles

The Leaves of the Divine Economy Model©

PREFACE

One of the beauties of the whole system is its reciprocity. Part of the wholesome environment that is sought comes from the health of the system itself. Leaves not only contribute to the growth but they also create a favorable microenvironment and eventually add nutrients back into the system, strengthening the roots. These real world economic principles are numerous like the leaves on a tree and their importance cannot be forgotten. Each leaf contributes in many ways to the overall health.

A CANOPY COMPOSED OF PRINCIPLES

With the foundation of the conceptual divine economy model laid out and production possibilities frontiers sufficiently examined it now becomes possible to insert economic principles into the model—fully aware of the interconnectedness of all of the principles. The locus of placement of the principles in the model is arbitrary yet it is logical. The logic of placement into the model can be deemed as a mental exercise, forcing one to examine just how interconnected the economic principles are. I take the liberty to begin the process.

To begin I divide the model into quadrants with a fundamental element on either side of each quadrant. Dividing the model into quadrants then sets the stage for examination of economic principles that have a strong tendency towards the following characteristics:

A. human spirit / order
B. order / transformation
C. transformation / law
D. law / human spirit.

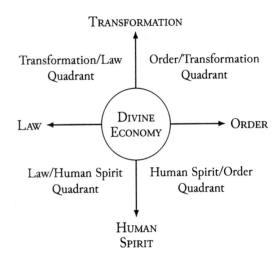

Diagram 4a: Quadrants of the Divine Economy Model ©

REAL WORLD ECONOMIC PRINCIPLES IN THE HUMAN SPIRIT / ORDER QUADRANT

I have chosen eight economic principles for placement in this quadrant. These are principles that exist in, emerge from, and complement both the human spirit and the social order. They find origin from human action and yet they also inspire more human action. They find expression in the market and are amplified in the market and at the same time they continuously emanate knowledge via the market. See Diagram 4b.

Price Theory

With regards price theory, a good starting point is the law of supply and demand. Accordingly, if the supply of a good or service increases,

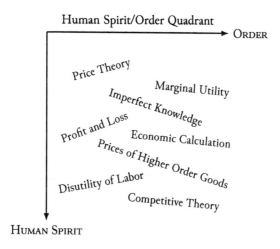

Diagram 4b: Economic principles in the human spirit/order quadrant

then the price decreases. Likewise if the demand for a good or service decreases, then the price decreases.

The price of a good or service in the real world is relative. It is relative to other goods and services and it is relative to the earlier price of that good or service itself which means that the system can be described as a floating price system. In other words, all prices are relative at the time and place of human action in the market. It is exactly that fact, that prices are relative to all others, that enables the price system to play an economizing role in decision-making.

Let us assume that you go to a marketplace with $100, needing food and clothing and medicine but you find the market in a dysfunctional state—there are no relative prices. Only one price, $45 for the clothing, is known at the time. Would you know how to prioritize, or whether to buy the clothing or not? A price system absent of relative prices strips the market process of its ability to function.

And now we have come to the point where there is a need to define the market to offset the commonly held prejudices against the market. The market is universal. It is a process where knowledge flows freely. The market is benevolent and its process is profoundly cooperative, and quietly consultative in nature.

The market is a conveyor of information just as is language. The following analogy is useful. Individually I can speak to myself alone or I can more fully use language and speak with others. Undoubtedly the full benefits of language as a human endowment come from its social nature. If I happen to speak vulgarly, language as a human institution should not be attacked as being harmful. In fact, the social nature of language empowers it to have a moderating and refining influence on individuals, thereby lessening the occurrence of vulgarity. The market, likewise, releases the full benefits of the human spirit and all of the associated resources. If someone acts in a crude or frivolous manner it is not the fault of the market. In fact it is the social nature of the market that will tend to moderate and refine individuals, ultimately facilitating the advancement of civilization.

The price system finds expression in the market in the form of relative prices which convey important information. For instance, factors which exhibit characteristics such as mobility or convertibility have a higher value than similar immobile or inconvertible factors. Here is another example: nominal wage rates mean little but real wage rates convey important information about wages since it is then put in terms that are relative to other prices. So even if all prices are decreasing but the wage rate is decreasing to a lesser degree then the real wage rate is actually increasing. The market is the vehicle for conveyance of this valuable information and people make decisions or choices based on it.

Business individuals active in the market assess costs and revenues and continually modify their plans due to the signals that come as a result of changes in demand and supply. These adjustments that are made as prices are influenced by demand and supply demonstrate that the price system is both dynamic and efficient.

Marginal Utility

Closely allied to relative prices is the concept of marginal utility. The market conveys information about the plethora of relative prices of goods and services but ultimately active decision-making by each person resides at the margin. The choice made is ultimately based on the subjective valuation about the perceived gain from the various choices. Whichever choice is perceived to bring the greatest satisfaction and fulfillment at the margin is chosen. Let us assume that I am very hungry and that I can buy either a pencil or an apple for a quarter. I will readily recognize the greater marginal utility of the apple and buy it.

Imperfect Knowledge

This is an insurmountable and an inescapable reality! As imperfect knowledge is moderated by having some knowledge and having some certainty people make decisions and act.

Part of the uncertainty comes from a lack of information, and the corollary to this is the uncertainty about the other human beings on the planet and their subjective decisions and their actions. The relatively free and immediate flow of knowledge that is the potential of the market ameliorates this condition. Another part of the uncertainty comes from the time element, that is, the great unknown we call the future. The only certainties are: that there are uncertainties, that the world is dynamic, and that the market works best when it is unhampered.

Profit and Loss

Concomitantly there is no certainty and therefore there is no guarantee that any effort made by a producer interacting in the market will yield a profit. It is a simple fact that all exchanges that take place during the market process occur because of a double inequality of values. Will an exchange take place? Exchange occurs only when both parties value what they receive higher than what they give.

Involvement as an entrepreneur has risk because of uncertainty. The nature of the active entrepreneur is to be alert to opportunities, that is to say, to needs not being met or not be being met as well as they could be. In the market it is possible that my perception as an entrepreneur is right or maybe it is wrong. It is possible that my perception of the resources that I happen to think are needed may combine to serve the consumer's wants better; or perhaps not.

This is a part of the constant ebb and flow that necessarily results from the uncertainty in the real world. The market encompasses all of the various facets of the economy, such as: profit and loss, entrepreneurship, communication, and knowledge; and the market conveys information in terms of relative prices.

In its earliest appearance in the primitive economy profit or loss was simply the outcome. If I raided a bird's nest I either found food or not. If my effort was not productive my failed effort represented my loss. If my effort was productive the food then profited me. The profit motive is a necessary and inherent feature of the human operating system. As humans evolved and as the economy evolved profits enabled producers 1) to provide wages and other factor incomes, and 2) to be one of the sources of the capital that encourages endeavors with lengthier production times.

Economic Calculation

Implied in the word 'calculation' is a basis of knowledge. It is then from this basis of knowledge that the next step—that of calculation—can proceed. Implied in the word 'economic' is information about the economy, which ultimately then is disseminated via the market.

But first things first! It just so happens that private property is an even more preliminary part of the market than the actual diffusion of knowledge. Values, of course, are necessary for calculation. Material and ideal 'things' are valued and are therefore sought after to be 'owned.' This 'value' is the basis of knowledge for calculation.

The economy is dynamic and composed of many trillions of needs and decisions that often change complexion. The basis of knowledge needed for economic calculation comes from the market in the form of relative prices. These prices are relative to all other prices at the current moment.

The freer the market is the quicker the information can flow and the greater the ability is for it to correct errors. Desires, needs, and resources converge in the market and find full expression in the form of relative prices. Economic calculation involves comparing and contrasting and speculating about the relative prices expressed through the market.

Any attempt to calculate economically using fictional non-market values—values arbitrarily assigned by someone removed from the market—ignores the dynamic nature of the knowledge within the market; which is tantamount to denying the human spirit. Use of non-market values is the reason why vertical production in an excessively large firm results in bureaucracy and calculation error, for instance.

This is also the reason why socialism fails, since it is an 'error-based institution.' What is meant by 'error-based' is the fact that the prices used for decision-making are arbitrary and imagined, not derived from the market process. These prices are erroneous and all decisions based on them are error-based.

Prices of Higher Order Goods

Not only does the market enable economic calculation but it extends beyond the here and now. The information in the market, the relative prices, also takes into account time. Goods which will reach the market in the future have a present value. And since they have value, so too, all of the resources needed in their production have value. In other words, factor prices also are relative prices.

However, without private property in factors of production there can be no realistic factor prices, and without factor prices cost accounting is impossible. To repeat, private property ownership is vital to the market. The economic calculation needed to realize profits, which pay the wages and factor incomes, depend on it. As decisions are made in the market—between consumer goods and higher order goods—a bridge forms between the present and the future. This bridging of the present and the future in the form of capital structure potentially leads to economic development.

Disutility of Labor

Exchange in the marketplace/market-process only happens if both parties feel that there is a gain. When an individual wishes to sell his services in the market he (she) checks to see what the relative prices (wages for example) are and then he must decide if the income is worth more than the alternatives, including leisure. What I mean by leisure is: whatever you would do instead of work if that was a choice that you could afford.

However, if leisure is subsidized in any way then less of the labor factor becomes available, which reduces the productive capacity of the economy and sends waves throughout the economy like ripples emanating from a pebble dropped in a pond. If leisure is subsidized then relative prices throughout the economy will change, leading to a cascading of aberrant decisions. Such is the plight and blight of the 'welfare economy.'

There is nothing wrong with disutility of labor determining whether there is an exchange in the market as long as it is a true expression rather than one distorted by subsidies. There is nothing wrong with the disutility of labor; in fact, the disutility of labor is actually a motive force. It inspires alertness to choices and alternatives. Indeed, disutility of labor underlies entrepreneurship and it also underlies capital.

Competitive Theory

The natural tendency for humans is to make progress. That is what is implied in the act of exchange since exchange only takes place when both parties perceive a gain. This searching and questing and striving is part of the human operating system. That is not to say that there is not disorder in the economy, like the example just given about the disorder resulting from subsidizing leisure.

Making decisions at the margin, based on the relativities, and comparing where you are with where you want to be is natural and it is a human quality. Striving for excellence and refining oneself and one's circumstances are meritorious expressions of this human trait. The knowledge that flows from the market-process provides the individual with 'data' in the form of relativities. Judgment about what is available, what possibilities exist, and about one's current condition, hinge on information available in the market.

Competition in the market is not a negative like it is in the animal world where 'survival of the fittest' is the outcome. The economy is divinely at the service of mankind. Competition in the market among producers leads to new and better goods and services and better means of production. With this advancing prosperity there are no long-run losers.

Currently, corruption of the divine economy by ego-driven manipulators directs wealth towards favored ones and away from others. This human intervention hampers the divine economy and is what causes 'the rich to get richer and the poor to get poorer.' In contrast to the hampered economy created by the interventionists, the net efficiencies that come from competition in a free market benefit everyone.

Human Spirit / Order Quadrant Example— Disutility of Labor

At a basic level each human being can distinguish between the ease or difficulty of the life task ahead. If a person is given the choice, that person will always prefer the easier of the two means of attaining their ends—as long as the task is not a recreational challenge or a personal development goal. What appears to be a non-productive urge—choosing the easy way—is actually a positive force. Disutility of labor is a sign of intelligence. It is a motivating force that leads to innovation. It inevitably causes advancement and progress.

Disutility of labor, despite being an underlying law of purposeful action, has been corrupted and turned into a negative characteristic in the economy under the current system of intervention. For instance, why work when your basic needs are met if you don't work? Or, why provide excellent service when you get paid the same either way, plus you cannot lose your job? These distortions caused by interventions pervert the inherent power of this economic law that is an inherent part of purposeful human action.

Human Spirit / Order Quadrant PPF Example

Developing production possibilities frontiers for each economic principle has never been done before! It requires contemplation and identification of the active principle and its antithesis. Let me take you through the thought process. A good place to start is to identify the meaning of the 'no growth' point. In this example—disutility of labor—the 'no growth' economy occurs when, in a relative sense, the aggregate satisfaction resulting from compensation for being non-productive equals the satisfaction resulting from compensation for being productive. See Diagram 4c.

If in aggregate the lack of productivity is rewarded the economy will contract as shown in Diagram 4d. This is why 'welfare economics' is counterproductive.

For those who say that 'welfare economics' is compassionate the end result is far from compassionate. A contracting economy, which inevitably results from this type of economic intervention, offers less goods and services, less employment, and lower standards of living. All

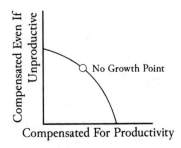

Diagram 4c: 'Disutility of labor' production possibilities frontier

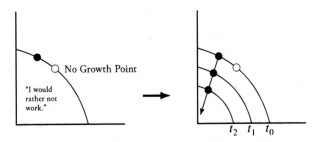

Diagram 4d: 'Disutility of labor' contracting economy

of this translates into increased human suffering so do not believe the 'so-called compassionate' ego-driven interventionists! See Diagram 4d.

Whereas this principle of the Human Spirit/Order Quadrant— disutility of labor as it occurs naturally in the divine economy—is an example of finding better ways to do things (Diagram 4e). Notably, it is where being productive is preferred over the tediousness of unproductive methods and habits.

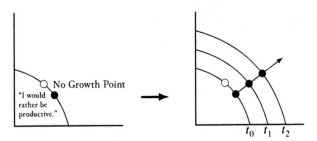

Diagram 4e: 'Disutility of labor' expanding economy

Summary of the Human Spirit / Order Quadrant

The market is a time and place where information about relative prices is discovered. It is also a process within which knowledge flows. Not all knowledge is expressed as a price, but all knowledge is relative, and it is the market where such knowledge is accessible to humans.

The market can be described as unplanned order. It is economic action in the market that creates wealth. For the sake of human enlightenment and for the sake of human prosperity the market needs to be unhampered. Human intervention in the market is inevitably a corruption and a disruption of the divine economy.

Selected Exercises

1. Find and describe a real world example for one of the specific principles in the Human Spirit/Order Quadrant.

2. Develop a series of production possibilities graphs that show 'no growth' and 'contracting' and 'expanding' economies for one Human Spirit/Order principle and describe the axes. Describe how the economy is affected if this economic principle is either understood or misunderstood.

REAL WORLD ECONOMIC PRINCIPLES IN THE ORDER / TRANSFORMATION QUADRANT

I have chosen nine economic principles for placement in this quadrant. These are the principles that find expression in and emerge from both the market and its capital structure. It is through the instrumentality of capital that the order of the market undergoes transformation. Equally symmetric and reciprocal is the vital need for the dynamic flow of information from within the market-process so that capital can exist and its structure can serve everyone's needs. See Diagram 4f.

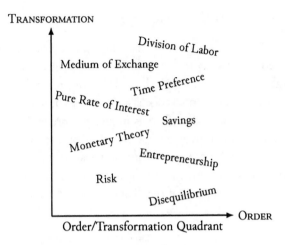

Diagram 4f: Economic principles in the order/transformation quadrant

Division of Labor

Without necessarily recognizing the concept of the division of labor, humans have operated according to this universal law. Praxeology, which can be defined as action logic, identified division of labor as a universal law of human action.

The moment a choice was made for the sake of efficiency there was division of labor no matter how primitive the historical culture. It is difficult to imagine even an early stage in the history of mankind when some degree of this law did not operate. It is as old as humanity itself and it is inseparable from humans.

These steps of efficiency and this production of wealth, this division of labor, is essentially the beginning of capital. Therefore it is a misconception to separate capital and labor since they are intricately interwoven, 'peas of the same pod,' and variations on the same theme.

Division of labor is expressed in the market as a type of social cooperation that comes from specialization—physical and intellectual specialization. The idea that the market process is quietly consultative in nature—which is a very high form of cooperation—implies that there is an intellectual division of labor, or in other words, specialization contained in the wisdom of each of the market-process participants. The increased wealth that results from division of labor provides incentive for such specialization.

The existence of division of labor indicates that there is a desire for more goods in the economy. Division of labor brings capital into existence, provides for diverse wisdom to enter the consultative market process, and it generates wealth which provides incentive for even more division of labor. It is an act of social cooperation. Mises concurs:

> In a hypothetical world in which the division of labor would not increase productivity, there would not be any society. There would not be any sentiments of benevolence and good will.[11, p. 145]

Medium of Exchange

As the division of labor continued and the economy evolved it was discovered that certain goods were basic to human well-being and therefore commonly sought after. Some of these basic goods were relatively less perishable and relatively easier to transport which made them valuable not only as a commodity but as a means of indirect exchange.

All over the world there were a myriad of mediums of exchange that emerged from different cultures. The most universally accepted medium of exchange that naturally emerged from the unhampered market was gold. It so happens—in contrast—that artificial mediums of exchange instituted by the interventionists are highly susceptible to corruption since they only exist because of a corruption of the natural processes of the divine economy to begin with.

Just as the market historically sifted through the alternative mediums of exchange and settled on gold, the test of a good medium of exchange is that it serves the economy and leads to further efficiencies. Confidence that it has value that cannot be destroyed makes it an effective economic means of traversing the time element. Overcoming this time element in the economy brings with it new and wonderful possibilities.

Once a medium of exchange is in place and universally accepted then all goods and services produced are valued in those terms. This was a major advancement since it made cost accounting possible. Both inputs and the goods and services produced were then in the same terms. From this point forward it was possible to evaluate and to determine profit and loss.

However if there is counterfeiting of the medium of exchange of any kind then the counterfeiters, who have not contributed anything to production, cause the exchange value of the money to decrease. Subsequently, the purchasing power of the money is negatively affected and it falls. The counterfeiters get something for nothing but the productive members of society are ultimately stolen from. This is true no matter who is the counterfeiter, the guy down the street or the central bank. Additionally, counterfeiting undermines the time element efficiency gains that come from having a perpetually good medium of exchange.

Time Preference

Time preference is the praxeological law that explains how humans value time. All humans prefer to have whatever good or service they need, now rather than later. They prefer to have the needed good now so if they have to wait then a premium is assigned to the good. The present good is equal to the same good in the future plus a premium.

Time preference is high or low but always positive. One way of understanding time preference is to recognize that there is always a 'cost' involved with saving until later rather than consuming in the present. It is either relatively high or relatively low. The higher the time preference the higher the discounting applied to the future. If people foresee war or fear for the future they will have a high time preference and will save less. In their eyes it is more costly to save.

If people foresee peace and prosperity on the horizon then they have a relatively low time preference and will be more willing to save. A lower time preference has a reciprocal effect, it brings about a higher degree of prosperity. Let us assume that I see good things on the horizon, like peace and trustworthiness. That makes me feel secure and confident about the future. As a result I will save if I have income greater than my current needs. My savings will then be used to advance prosperity.

Pure Rate of Interest

The premium assigned to future goods relative to the same goods in the present would represent the pure rate of interest at the individual level. The collective expression of this valuation for each culture is the pure rate of interest. The only way to get a sense of this expression of the cultural time preference is in the market since all real signals are sent within the market. What you find in the market is the market interest rate—which is the pure rate of interest, plus a premium to compensate for the risk incurred over time for the particular endeavor, plus a factor (that is often underestimated) which is an attempt to account for the changes in the purchasing power of the money if the money is being corrupted.

To get a realistic snapshot of the market rate of interest we look at the demand and supply of loanable funds. The amount of loanable funds available represents the supply side. The demand for loanable funds intersects the supply of loanable funds determining the market clearing price, which approximates the pure rate of interest. In brief, in an unhampered economy time preference is a major determinant of the supply of loanable funds and the demand for these loanable funds by entrepreneurs represents the demand side. See Diagram 4g.

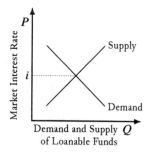

Diagram 4g: Market interest rate and loanable funds in an unhampered economy

Savings

The time element of the economy causes befuddlement among economists and non-economists alike. Savings is simply the allocation of income over time. Most understand that income is allocated among various goods and services in the present. For example, I spend some of my income on housing, food, clothing and entertainment, and that is understood. Expanding on this thought, now in addition to these I also allocate a portion of my income to a time horizon that extends into the future. This is savings. Savings then translates in the economy as loanable funds. The befuddled ones miss this point.

Economic growth is limited by loanable funds. Savings is simply another way of saying loanable funds. It is true that wealthier individuals have a larger portion of their income, in absolute and perhaps as a percentage of the total of their income, directed into some form of savings. These are the funds that people have willingly made available for use, in exchange for a rate of return based on their time preferences. Now, regardless of the current stock of savings and investment, the key to economic development is new and additional savings which releases new capital for use by entrepreneurs in already established and new productive efforts. This is what is meant by economic growth.

The market absorbs and conveys information about the present plus it conveys all of the time element information as perfectly well as is possible. Essentially, the market is in divine order.

It is one thing for the befuddled ones to miss the point that savings is simply an allocation of income over time, but it is quite another and more sinister thing for the befuddled ones to then impose acts of intervention on the market due to their ignorance of what savings is. An example of this would be lowering interest rates to encourage consumption and discourage savings. This act of interference is done because the interveners regard savings as the absence of consumption rather than as the conscious choice to consume at a later time. Intervention into this part of the economy, directed towards reducing savings, is extremely disruptive and it is destructive of capital.

Monetary Theory

Money is a medium of exchange that permits indirect exchange and brings about all the resulting efficiencies. Give consideration to these efficiencies by contrasting them with the awkwardness and impracticality of having to barter each and every time you wished to make an exchange.

One of the defining and determining qualities used when human societies chose its medium of exchange was the stock of money. Typically the medium of exchange was neither superabundant nor was it extremely rare. However once the medium of exchange is adopted in the market, because of its superior qualities and its performance as a medium of exchange, the stock of money is a non-factor. One stock of money is as good as another. If the demand for money increases it simply causes the value of each unit of money to increase.

Prices of all goods and services are in terms of money so the relativities expressed in the market are maintained, which means that the market functions as always, conveying information about the relative prices of goods and services. The divine economy equilibrates quickly and it instantaneously adjusts itself to each market interaction regardless of the stock of money.

The stock of money circulates in the present and connects the present to the future through savings. Savings represents loanable funds which becomes capital. Capital is what enables people to get paid now for their present services even though the 'end of the line' fruit of their work does not make it to the market until some time in the future.

The medium of exchange that is chosen in the divine economy— due to its merits—is universally and voluntarily accepted, partially because it cannot be manipulated artificially. One such example is gold. In other words, no amount of alchemy can create gold out of thin air, which means that there is no such thing as a business cycle in the divine economy. God does not play games with the economy or with mankind. However, the interventionists are playing a monetary game with the economy by manipulating the stock of money. One of the most visible consequences of their intervention is the repeated occurrence of a business cycle. It is the mismanagement of the monetary system by ego-driven interventionists that causes these business cycles.

Entrepreneurship

The spirit of entrepreneurship is uniquely human. It is the quality of being alert to possibilities. It is the driving force in the economy and it has origins in the disutility of labor. Even though all human beings possess various degrees of capacity for entrepreneurship most of the time for most people it is only a potential, resting in latency.

It is the interactions that take place in the market, the sparks of information there, which activate entrepreneurship. The most active entrepreneurs intentionally go to the market in an alert state methodi- cally seeking arbitrage or other opportunities. They systematically seek prospective differences between revenues and costs in excess of the natural interest rate, taking into consideration price expectations. Some active entrepreneurs just happen to be at the right place at the right time but afterwards quickly return to latency.

There is some active entrepreneurship that is a response to a 'gut feeling' and some that comes from systematic calculation. Both are responses to opportunities perceived from the market information. The chances of success—yielding a profit rather than a loss—are greater when the entrepreneur has systematically examined the possibilities for profit or loss before taking action.

Regardless of whether it comes about from relative novices or experienced entrepreneurs the market process is driven forward by entrepreneurship. Opportunities are sought after and found. As described by Kirzner:

> The entrepreneur's activity is essentially competitive. And this competition is inherent in the nature of the entrepreneurial market process. Or, to put it the other way around, entrepreneurship is inherent in the competitive market process.[5, pp. 16–17]

None of this happens in a risk-free world of certainty. In fact the exact opposite is the reality. What an entrepreneur may discover to be an opportunity may never materialize. What seems like good timing may fail in real time. Or to the contrary, the timing and magnitude and location of an endeavor may indeed satisfy the wants and needs of consumers significantly more—just as alertly discerned. Profits and losses are regulating forces and both are inherent in the market. A market that is uncorrupted by intervention—that is, a free market— allows the entrepreneur to most clearly perceive the signals needed to serve all of our needs.

Risk

Risk is an inevitable part of the economy because there is uncertainty and imperfect knowledge. But there are market equilibrating forces that moderate risk. Savings, for one, serves to mollify risk since savings can be used to meet an immediate need or it can be directed toward production for the future. If risk is of an actuarial nature then purchasing insurance will lead to a reduction of risk.

Entrepreneurs take on the role of major risk-takers and relieve others of that burden. Additionally, there is the likelihood that many of the entrepreneurs are skillful and have gained wisdom from their experiences, which skews risk towards success, lessening the degree of risk. For instance, entrepreneurs skillfully calculate economically using market information about relative prices, revenues and costs, and the availability of capital, which adds systemization and discipline to the decision-making process.

Finally, the level of charity that a society has reduces risk accordingly. If people care about one another they will give assistance when the unpredictable leads to misfortune. This lessens the risk for those affected by dire circumstances.

There is enough uncertainty and risk in the economy without more being created by the interventionists. The claim is made by those who interfere with the economy that they are reducing risk. What that actually means is that they are trying to reduce the risk for some particular favored group.

These ignorant or ego-driven interventionists do not and cannot fathom all of the negative consequences that result from their acts of interference with the market forces. Their disruption of the market process, in and of itself, increases risk for everyone, even the "protected' and favored groups. Everything becomes riskier in a hampered economy since the flow of knowledge is impeded.

Disequilibrium

The fact that there is always uncertainty and imperfect knowledge implies that the economy is constantly in flux. Errors are inherent but fleeting; are followed by fleeting inherent errors again, and so on and so on. The equilibrating forces that operate in the market—one of them being entrepreneurship—constantly purge errors.

The forces underlying demand and supply move the economy towards equilibrium. Never is the economy in equilibrium but it is always tending towards it. Disequilibrium, with powerful tendencies toward equilibrium, is the norm. If errors persist and linger that indicates that the error has become institutionalized and to some degree impermeable to market forces. All institutionalized errors are caused by human intervention and prevent the full expression of the divine potentials of the economy.

Order / Transformation Quadrant Example—Savings

Let us examine the difference between human savings and the savings of a squirrel. Apparently both anticipate the future! The squirrel's action is very strongly driven by instinct; however if environmental conditions change significantly the squirrel will modify the size of its cache. Likewise, human savings will be modified as a consequence of conditions. Human intelligence, which can span time conceptually and which can unravel the numerous and various complexities of the world, enables humans to save purposefully. Simply stated, savings is a productive and vital aspect of life.

Under the current system of economic intervention, the proponents of intervention come to the bizarre conclusion that savings is harmful. For example, Keynesian economics—a variant of which underlies the predominant economic systems practiced worldwide—demonizes people's choice to save. Their forced incentives to diminish savings is like force-feeding the squirrels this year only to find that their essential cache for the future is completely gone, ultimately leading to disaster.

Order / Transformation Quadrant PPF Example

Since this example (savings/dissavings) is so similar to the one (the consumption/investment PPF) used when I introduced the production possibilities frontier concept in Chapter 3, I will select a different principle—different from savings—to use as the example for this quadrant. Let's look at entrepreneurship. See Diagram 4h.

The 'no growth' point is where the potential of alertness is offset by distorted signals. As more and more economic signals are distorted the economy contracts as shown in Diagram 4i.

In an expanding economy the chances of successful entrepreneurship increase because the signals are real, and vice versa, since the signals are real the chances of successful entrepreneurship are greater. See Diagram 4j.

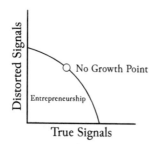

Diagram 4h: 'Entrepreneurship' production possibilities frontier

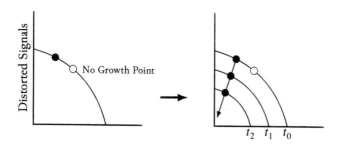

Diagram 4i: 'Entrepreneurship' contracting economy

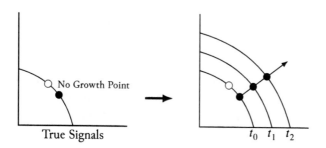

Diagram 4j: 'Entrepreneurship' expanding economy

Summary of the Order / Transformation Quadrant

Born from the womb of the economy are such specializations as division of labor and medium of exchange. Unborn—time seamlessly connects the present and the future economy via the price known as the pure interest rate. Savings, or the supply of loanable funds, is available to be used for economic development by entrepreneurs who see discrepancies in relative prices in the present and over extended time periods. It is discernment of the interactions within the market process that transforms from latent to active each hopeful entrepreneur. Human intervention into the market distorts market signals and causes dire consequences in the present and in the future. These distortions, at least the ones stemming from artificial interest rates, are called malinvestments.

Selected Exercises

1. Develop an 'Example' for one of the specific principles, other than savings, in the Order/Transformation Quadrant.

2. Identify what the 'no growth' point represents for each of the nine principles in the Order/Transformation Quadrant.

Real World Economic Principles in the TRANSFORMATION / LAW Quadrant

I have chosen eight economic principles for placement in this quadrant. These eight principles demonstrate reciprocal action within the continuum bounded on one side by capital and on the other by property rights. This is a fascinating quadrant since it attempts to bridge the role of capital as it transmutes and transforms, with the non-transmutable nature of the law of human rights. See Diagram 4k.

Willingness to Work

If we assume that there is no coercion then the first order of incentive for the human being is to meet one's own needs. Since it is possible to meet

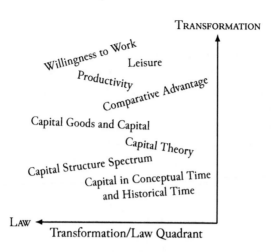

Diagram 4k: Economic principles in the transformation/law quadrant

one's own needs by taking action; that is what is done. What we acquire from our labor we are able to keep, presumably. It can be deduced that this basic property right is necessary and sufficient to make a person willing to work.

A negative corollary is that without the right to receive the fruits of one's labor there would be an unwillingness to work. Nothing destroys the willingness to work faster than removing the human right to 'reap what you sow.'

Leisure

Leisure is having the time to appreciate any wealth above basic subsistence. Leisure describes the circumstance that exists once all vital needs are met and a choice is then made to refrain from work to pursue something more pleasurable. Consider the significance of leisure. Not only does the transformation of labor into property give an incentive to work but acquisition of even a most rudimentary property right—here given as time to rest—gives one the right to make choices. As soon as there are choices there is the potential for leisure, for division of labor, for active entrepreneurship, and for the emergence of capital.

Productivity

The more productive one is the more property rights one acquires. The more property rights one has the more choices there are, which further cascades into more loci for entrepreneurial action and more diverse types of capital investments.

Technological innovation springs from these diverse types of capital investments. Guess what? All of these lead to increased productivity. Productivity, then, is an expression of individual initiative and it leads to increased real wages.

Operating within this milieu is the productive actions of businessmen and the users of capital and it is their actions that generate profits. A portion of these profits then goes towards new capital in the form of wages and factor incomes. Businessmen and women and the users of capital play a guiding role, as stated by Mises:

> What produces the product are not toil and trouble in themselves, but the fact that the toiling is guided by reason. The human mind alone has the power to remove uneasiness.[11, p. 142]

This advancing productivity is thoroughly described by Reisman:

> The precise nature of the work of businessmen and capitalists needs to be explained. In essence, it is to raise the productivity, and thus the real wages, of manual labor by means of creating, coordinating, and improving the efficiency of the division of labor.[6]

The cascading continues. If I am more productive then my real wage will increase which translates into more savings provided the future is perceived as hopeful. This will create new capital which will be used to increase productivity.

Increased productivity can be defined as more consumer goods per productive unit. As the supply of goods increases the price of those goods decreases, which means an increase in the standard of living in real terms. What can be discerned from this is that property rights, which underlie productivity, serve as the foundation for development. Once the connection between property rights and productivity is understood a new work ethic will emerge.

Comparative Advantage

Comparative advantage is a derivation of the concept of relativity. Regardless of absolute advantage every person or geographic unit has a comparative advantage with regards some good or service relative to their trading partners. Trade occurs only if both sides benefit, implying that there is a double inequality in exchange. Both trade partners value what they get more than what they trade away.

Comparative advantage is also a derivative of the division of labor. Trading partners will divide their labors so that each is producing and trading the good or service that enables both sides to maximize their benefit from trade. This specialization from division of labor, combined with the secondary benefits that come from both trading and from maintaining a base of productive capacity, is what captures the benefits of comparative advantage.

The resources that are uniquely mine as part of my skill set and my property rights are such that I have a comparative advantage with regards something, relative to my trading partners' skills and property rights. If we engage in trade, the fact that we do trade means that we both have gained. Therefore the gain is in some degree an advancement which then can be consumed or otherwise used to expand my property rights —possibly into capital goods—either directly or indirectly through savings. To take full advantage of the opportunities that come from trade (exchange) I will specialize in producing the good or service in which I have the relative (comparative) advantage.

Capital Goods and Capital

These are intermediate goods or producer goods which make it possible for consumer goods and services to be made more readily available and/or of higher quality. Capital goods initially require the use of capital to pay those making or using the capital goods until there is a flow of income from the 'end of the line' consumer good or service. It is easy to see that capital structurally exists in different stages of development. Some capital goods are already completed and are producing goods. Other capital is tied up in capital goods which still are not completed and still are not producing goods.

Capital is a loan of the fruits of past labor. The users of capital—capitalists—pay for the factors needed, either as wages or as factor incomes (to factors other than labor), as part of the production process. These wages and factor incomes are costs to the capitalist.

If the returns to capital are greater than the costs of capital then the capital value increases. Additionally, if new or free capital becomes available it is alertly used since capital is the most limiting factor in the economy. Capital originates from loanable funds, that is, from savings. Just as economic growth is limited by capital, consumption is limited by production. Notice the sequence for an advancing economy: savings then capital then production of goods and services for consumption.

Something that has to be addressed: there is a severe prejudice towards the word 'capitalist.' The historical reason for this prejudice is outside the scope of this book. In the divine economy the capitalist is seen as a real and vital agent of the economy just like time is a vital element or entrepreneurs are vital agents, or just like property rights are considered as vital.

This book makes it clear repeatedly that there is a great deal of ignorance about economics and so there are many prejudices to be overcome. Mises broadens the view when addressing productive capital:

> Production is not something physical, material, and external; it is a spiritual and intellectual phenomenon. Its essential requisites are not human labor and external natural forces and things, but the decision of the mind to use these factors as means for the attainment of ends. [11, p. 142]

Education is a type of capital. The education that is necessary for remedying the problems of economic prejudice and ignorance will not come from institutions that are funded by the interventionists. This book is one of the ways to gain clarity about economics, independent of contemporary prejudices.

Capital Theory

Of all the factors in the economy capital is the most limiting. Why? Look back at the sections about loanable funds and time preference. People strongly prefer things in the present. Therefore even under the most peaceful conditions only a small proportion of their incomes will be saved. Whereas the other half of the loanable funds market is the demand for loanable funds; and that is a function of what can be described as an intense and determined search for capital in the market.

Capital is the most limiting factor in the economy because it is constrained by loanable funds. The economy is also most limited by capital since capital is the transformational element of the economy which, of course, would make it highly sought after. Remember the earlier discussion about the efficiency gain that comes from division of labor. Well, it is capital that yields a cumulative and collective efficiency gain for the economy that dwarfs all of the other economic factors. Capital is the key to progress.

Once the primitive economy moved beyond individuals being self-sufficient but barely subsistent, capital became the means of payment to labor and other factors used in the production of goods. In reality there is no rivalry between labor and capital except in the fictional model of the world imagined by Marx and those who are like-minded, where capital is selectively excluded from the economy. Labor is intimately and ultimately the beneficiary of capital just as are the owners of the other factors of production.

Let us consider the economically relevant subject of the formation of capital. Here, disutility of labor is a motivating element, as is time preference (which determines the level of savings). Refer to the interactive three-way relationship in Diagram 4l. Division of labor, a specialization that is an expression of human diversity, creates in the market loci for arbitrage and profit opportunities. This quickly draws the attention of alert entrepreneurs. Savings are then used as capital by the entrepreneurs to pay the wages and factor incomes until the time when revenues can. Sales revenue minus the money costs (wages and factor incomes) eventually yields a profit (or a loss). Some of the net income then re-enters

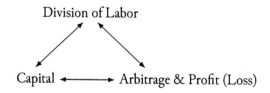

Diagram 4l: Interactive three-way relationship

as loanable funds, that is, as 'new' capital. Entrepreneurial alertness also contributes to the identification of ways to specialize, combining with capital to augment the division of labor. See Diagram 4l.

Another interesting economic benefit from capital is the actual generation of information about both revenues and costs as a result of the application of capital in the economy. It is the involvement in the economy by capitalists that creates wages and factor prices (these are their costs) and sales revenues. These wage and factor prices serve as a source of information, enabling entrepreneurs and capitalists to calculate so they can make rational decisions. If we assume these decisions are from the market signals in a divine economy (in other words, in an unhampered, free market, laissez-faire economy), they are fully compatible with the divine concepts of unity and justice.

In a 'Crusoe' situation—one person isolated on an island—the initial payment for his initial work (his wage) equals his profit. He works by climbing a coconut tree and he eats the coconut (profit). At that point the wage to profit ratio is equal to one. Once there is an opportunity to specialize (trading with others in a market) and there is savings, capital enters into the scenario which potentially generates wages and factor incomes. To see how capital benefits labor, refer to Diagram 4m. Notice the intricacies that make up the economic definition of an ever-advancing economy.

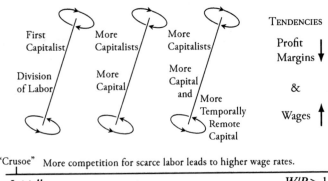

Diagram 4m: Capital benefits labor

If there are profits then that will end up creating 'new' savings. New savings means more capital which attracts those seeking capital. As the number of capitalists increases wages and factor incomes increase because there is competition for these scarce resources which puts upward pressure on the wages and factor prices.

Division of labor at the early stages near 'Crusoe' was crude but as it is directed by businessmen and capitalists, division of labor becomes more refined. The process continues. Generation of wealth not only brings more capitalists to the market but it also leads to an expansion of the use of capital to more productive, temporally remote production processes.

As the number of capitalists increases the profits tend to decrease, with each getting a smaller portion, independent of the wages and factor incomes paid out during production. In other words, wages and factor incomes tend to increase while profits tend to decrease. Additionally, every innovation and improvement that comes from this process ultimately reaches the consumers who benefit from both better products and lower prices brought about by innovation. In summary, the wage to profit ratio (W/P) increases as civilization advances.

There is a tendency toward a uniform rate of return on all capital invested which closely approximates the pure rate of interest. Mises makes a similar observation:

> The history of mankind is the record of a progressive intensifi-
> cation of the division of labor—The operation of the principle
> of division of labor and its corollary, cooperation, tends ulti-
> mately toward a world-embracing system of production.[10,
> p. 234-5]

Business cycles do not occur in the divine economy since none of the signals in the market are distorted. The market interest rate truly reflects the amount of savings that people have, creating a balance throughout the capital structure between the present and the future. When an artificial interest rate is created by the deceitful practices associated with fiat currencies the entrepreneurs allocate capital incorrectly—in both the amount invested and the capital invested temporally across the time horizon—which leads to a business cycle.

If we make an assumption—that there is only a single act of intervention—then all the malinvestments would be purged by the divine economy during the passage of one business cycle. But since resources are allocated across a span of time and across a spectrum of capital structure, a business cycle is not merely something that happens at one specific point in time. The negative consequences manifest themselves over many time periods or until all the malinvestments are purged for the duration of that cycle.

If consumer credit is extended in the market artificially, which means that it is unmatched by existing savings, capital is consumed. What is happening is that consumption is in excess of the productive capacity. Productive capacity in the economy is supported by the level of savings and the subsequent capital. The only way to now consume more is to use current savings, which was to serve as the loanable funds for 'new' capital and economic growth. This is the equivalent of consuming capital which consequently will cause the economy to regress, the typical consequence of intervention.

The important point to note here is that the divine economy heals itself and cannot be destroyed. All disruption and disorder in the economy comes from corruption caused by human intervention. Equilibrating forces begin to clear these afflictions almost immediately after intervention is halted. Rest assured that the power of the divine economy is indestructible and self-healing.

Capital Structure Spectrum

Production of all types requires capital. Some capital may be needed for a short time like a day or a week or a month. Other capital needs to suffice production for years. The picture that emerges is a wide array of production, funded for varying lengths of time, all of which makes up the capital structure funded by savings.

The starting point of an endeavor is very significant. If there is plenty of capital available at the beginning then the scale of production can be of a greater magnitude. Likewise, if there is plenty of capital the temporal remoteness from the consumer good can be greater. In other words, there can be more research and development when capital is relatively plentiful, which ultimately makes the possible fruits of that endeavor greater.

The concept of originary interest[11, p. 526] is closely related to time preference but it can be used to explain a different aspect of the economy. Originary interest is another of the praxeological laws that describes how humans act. People act in such a way that demonstrates that they value present goods higher than those same goods in the future, in relative terms.

In and of itself originary interest explains why people take action in the present. Without this conceptual reality operating in the human psyche there would be no consumption since there would be no preference for anything now. Humans devoid of originary interest would have no motivation to eat now, in the present, which would cause the species to go extinct. Needless to say, human beings do, indeed, place a high valuation on the present.

After considering all of these points it becomes clear that capital structure is really a spectrum. The most immediate end of the spectrum is current consumption: say, ice cream about to be selected from the freezer at the store. The more roundabout means of production, those that are temporally remote from the consumer, are located towards the other end of the spectrum. Capital is heterogeneous and inherent, beginning with consumption goods at the most immediate end of the capital structure spectrum. See Diagram 4n.

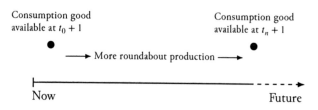

Diagram 4n: Fruits of the capital structure spectrum

The capital structure spectrum is a conceptual representation of the various fruits of capital (consumption goods) over time. This idea of one spectrum for all the various forms or structures of capital serves as another proof of the inseparability of capital from the consumption choices made to sustain and satisfy life. There is nothing evil about capital, in fact, capital is simply a vital element of the economy.

Capital in Conceptual Time and in Historical Time

When there appears to be no time other than the present ($t = 0$) the originary interest tells us that all consumption would be immediate. There would be no savings. When the time horizon expands ($t + 1$) the originary interest tells us that priority is given to the present time but that a pool of funding will begin to form unless, that is, the economy is in a primitive condition of basic subsistence. Of course the concept of time implies that there is a future. Thus, conceptual time shows that capital inevitably forms.

When the economy began in its simplest form, which let's say occurred at $t = 0$, the effort made just for survival meant that the gain (profit) was equivalent to the compensation for the labor (wage). In other words, the hunger was satisfied or the thirst was quenched. As the economy evolved ($t + 1$) and progressed past subsistence due to the development of division of labor, capital became available to pay wages and factor incomes (money costs) and the capital structure formed. Then the 'revenues minus costs' information brought about the ability to calculate which then enabled entrepreneurs to drive the economy forward. Historical time shows that capital emerges and serves to continually increase the wage-to-profit ratio. Notably, labor and productive factors are the beneficiaries of capital.

Transformation / Law Quadrant Example— Comparative Advantage

Comparative advantage operates in human society because human beings are complex and they have a plethora of needs and wants. To some extent geographic distances act as a limitation. Since there are numerous trading partners with a great diversity of special skills and talents, all of whom also have a great number of needs, the law of comparative advantage operates without fail.

This law can be violated causing great harm to all and especially to those whose alternatives are the most limited. One example of intervention that does this type of damage is any kind of trade barrier, for example, tariffs. A regional, simple economy may need to have free access to markets for their comparative advantage to be realized. Tariffs may destroy the feasibility of its comparative advantage, depriving this simple regional economy of the ability to transform itself. Without such interference the law of comparative advantage would activate all the agents of prosperity: division of labor, then trade, and possibly savings, capital, and entrepreneurship—that is, if we assume that property rights exist.

Transformation / Law Quadrant PPF Example

The 'no growth' point in this example (Comparative Advantage) is where free trade and division of labor are offset (negated) by trade barriers. See Diagram 4o.

Diagram 4o: 'Comparative advantage' production possibilities frontier

As more trade barriers are raised there is less ability to take advantage of the division of labor. The result is a contracting economy. See Diagram 4p.

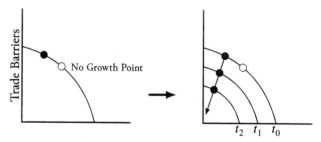

Diagram 4p: 'Comparative advantage' contracting economy

Free trade increases the division of labor which leads to wealth-generating specialization and capital formation. In this environment the economy expands. See Diagram 4q.

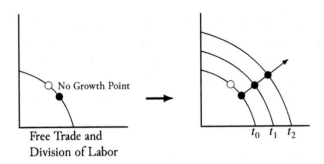

Diagram 4q: 'Comparative advantage' expanding economy

Summary of the Transformation / Law Quadrant

The divine economy rests firmly on property rights. In contrast, what suffers most in an economy hampered by weak property rights is people's willingness to save and the ability for capital to accumulate. The economy then loses its power to transform. The divine economy has an intricate capital structure which acts as an agent of transformation leading to economic development. Built into the divine economy are all the incentives that encourage movement towards more choices and towards the use of capital.

Selected Exercises

1. Identify the 'no growth' points for each of the eight principles in the Tranformation/Law quadrant. Compare them in a simultaneous equations format and come to at least one conclusion.

   Examples of simultaneous equations:

   From last section:
   Entrepreneurship + True Signals = Expanding Economy

   From this section:
   Free Trade + Division of Labor = Expanding Economy

2. Now state the conclusion that you arrived at in exercise one in terms of a non-interventionist policy.

Real World Economic Principles in the
Law / Human Spirit Quadrant

I have chosen five economic principles for placement in this quadrant. See Diagram 4r. What we have here is the blending of the human spirit as it operates according to the universal laws inherent in the human operating system; blended with a legal framework that is based on the divine principle of justice. At the heart of the divine economy is the transcendental property right—transcendental because there is no real separation between property rights and human rights. As presented by Rothbard:

> In the first place, there are senses in which property rights are identical with human rights: one, that property can only accrue to humans, so that their rights to property are rights that belong to human beings; and two, that the person's right to his own body, his personal liberty, is a property right in his own person as well as a 'human right.' [7, p. 113]

All the various forms of human rights are merely different types of property rights and serve as a protection of the human spirit. Enforcement of law is within its proper bounds when it is limited to the defense of person and property against all types of violent and coercive intervention.

Diagram 4r: Economic principles in the law/human spirit quadrant

Private ownership of the means of production benefits everyone since the fruits of those means of production go to everyone via the market. This is part of a continuous and progressive process and it translates into what can be described as a rising standard of living. Prosperity, which can be defined as an ever-improving standard of living for everyone, is the outcome of exercising property rights in an unhampered market.

Subjective Valuation

Each person is unique and has unique interests—that is, both in the array of interests and the degree of interests. Each choice made is a reflection of that person's subjective valuation.

Subjective valuations do not have an empirical nature to them. There is no number that represents your like or dislike of an orange. Nor is there a need for such a representation since the market perfectly handles each subjective choice instantaneously and in conjunction with all the other relative and subjective choices. Subjective valuation is a human right emanating from the human spirit.

Consumer Sovereignty

Human beings are created noble, created in the image of God. The world and all of its wonders are for the glory and exaltation of humanity. In the end, all things in this world serve mankind. When a desire is manifested as a choice there is an opportunity for some of the resources of the world to be directed towards meeting that desire.

In a sense all forces are mobilized to answer the command of the king—the consumer. The entrepreneur, by nature, is alert to these opportunities and perceives the signals sent in the market. The motion set in order by the entrepreneur moves resources towards whatever means are needed to satisfy the consumer—the king.

Production of goods and services to satisfy the king—the consumer —necessitates that the producers hire labor and other resources. This consumer oriented production employs people directly or indirectly. In that way all of the 'subjects' benefit from the producers' service to the 'king.'

Wherever in the economy the consumers spend more the profits rise and this stimulates economic competition; followed by specific investment and production. In other words, the pattern of investment and production follows the consumer spending pattern, in obedience to the 'king.'

What if a righteous person notices that the consumers are choosing foolish things? Although the divine economy is always in operation, the degree of the maturity of humanity is always in a state of imperfection. The present position of the ever-advancing economy along the spiritual maturity spectrum (Diagram 4s) is due to the state of perfection that mankind has reached and due to the amount of hindrance of the divine economy by intervention. Relative to the future humanity at the present is immature, but relative to the past humanity is advancing toward higher ideals and values. See Diagram 4s.

Ever-Advancing Economy

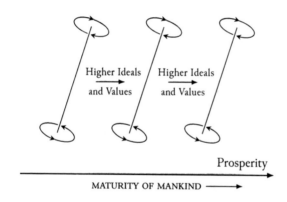

Diagram 4s: Maturity of mankind

The divine economy is not to be blamed for the present shortcomings evident in humankind. Instead, intervention needs to be removed so that information can flow freely and so that the divine virtues inherent in human beings can be more readily discovered and 'acquired' and polished.

Purchasing Power of Money

Money is the medium of exchange that enables the benefits of indirect exchange to permeate the market. It has value relative to all the other goods in the economy. The value of the money that I possess is my property, in other words, it is a property right of mine. If I can expect to get 2 pounds of sugar for one dollar but instead, surreptitiously, I receive only one pound it is clear that there has been a theft. The equivalent value of fifty cents was quietly taken from me.

Likewise if the money is debased by deliberate actions, everyone who uses the money is a victim. Stealing incrementally from everyone who uses the money (and necessarily in ways that favor those with ties to the interventionists) does not make such an act, the debasement of the money, a just act by any righteous definition.

The value of money finds its real definition in the market relative to other goods and services but it is based on the demand for money and the supply of money. If there is the ability to print money (counterfeiting and central bank inflation, as examples), then by increasing the supply of money without respecting the property rights of all those who have money, the purchasing power of money—its value—will decline. All holders of money will then have their property rights violated.

Contracts

The purpose of contracts is to provide a legal framework for protecting private property and market operations. The gains from trade and exchange extend into the economy by the ensuring of both payments and delivery as accorded by contracts. This contractual protection of private property encourages savings and the accretion of capital across the time horizon which raises the standard of living for everyone.

Ownership: There can be only one person (or any of the larger business entities of ownership) that has the exclusive rights to a particular physical piece of property at the same time.

Rent and Interest: Ownership of land or of a durable good or of loanable funds confers the right to portion it out to others and to charge them for its use. Ownership does not necessarily equate with use. Use does not define ownership.

Insurance: The providers of this type of contract define the risk groups and discriminate between risk groups and establish a contractual relationship with the client based on actuarial data.

Standard of Living

A standard of living needs to be measured in real terms, not in nominal terms. In real terms the standard of living increases as capital increases and as division of labor takes place. To see how capital, incrementally new capital, leads to an improved standard of living refer to Diagram 4t. In other words, as productivity increases real wages increase even while market competition is pushing the economy towards a uniform rate of return on capital.

Ever-Advancing Economy
(Also Showing How It Is Interfered With By Intervention)

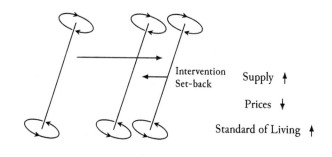

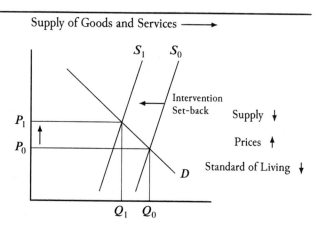

Diagram 4t: Capital advances standard of living but intervention does not

Now here is the vision of the standard of living that is possible in an unhampered economy, the divine economy. As capital increases productivity increases, which causes the supplies of goods and services to increase, thus causing their prices to decrease. And since productivity is increasing, in turn, real wages are increasing which means, overall, that the standard of living is increasing. As the standard of living increases the perception of hope and prosperity increases which means that the time preference lowers. A lower time preference translates into more savings which brings us back to the beginning stage of this 'standard of living' cycle: that is, an increase in capital resulting from an increase in savings. Notice the trends—capital increases productivity, prices decrease, real income increases, the standard of living increases and prosperity increases. (Contemplate the ever-advancing economy by studying Diagrams 4m, 4s and 4t.)

Increases in nominal wage rates without increases in productivity (which occurs in a hampered economy) are attributed to inflation of the money supply and this anomaly can be traced back to the interventionists. In the long run the standard of living decreases in real terms despite nominal increases. In other words, the supply of goods and services do not increase while prices do increase, because of inflation, which lowers the standard of living. See Diagram 4t.

Law / Human Spirit Quadrant Example— Subjective Valuation

The divine economy rests on the foundation that each and every human being is created in the image of God and that each one is unique. Unique in the sense that there are no two alike, never were and never will be. How could there be anything other than subjective valuation in the human realm, then, by definition? If we are all different in the array of qualities of spirit and fabric then necessarily we will always intellectually function subjectively.

This is not a problem scientifically as long as the proper methodology is used. Applying the objective methodology of the natural sciences, as if we operate like atoms within a molecule, is inappropriate. Many of the economic fallacies, today propagated as economic facts, were derived from trying to use an objective methodology upon a creature which is subjective by nature.

Only the subjective methodology can accommodate free will. Free will is another foundational piece of the divine economy since all of the actors in the economy have free will. Free will is also a foundation of the creation of humankind; it is part of human nature. It manifests itself in the independence of each decision made within the mind of each person—which is subjective valuation. Each decision is unique to the circumstances deemed important by each individual, who are themselves unique and therefore subjective.

Law / Human Spirit Quadrant PPF Example

The 'no growth' point in the subjective valuation production possibilities frontier is where creative gains, in aggregate, are offset by the stifling that comes from restricted choices. See Diagram 4u.

Diagram 4u: 'Subjective valuation' production possibilities frontier

As free will is restricted and as subjective valuation is unappreciated the economy contracts. See Diagram 4v.

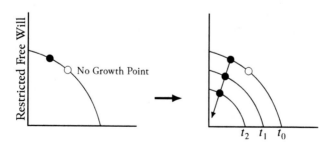

Diagram 4v: 'Subjective valuation' contracting economy

As non-violent free will is honored the information about what people value becomes known in the market and subsequently the economy expands. See Diagram 4w.

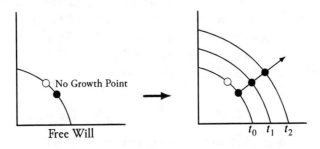

Diagram 4w: 'Subjective valuation' expanding economy

Summary of the Law / Human Spirit Quadrant

The really important part of this quadrant of the model is that there is a link to law: laws that provide a legal framework to support property rights; and laws of human action. The legal framework that supports property rights recognizes the importance of contracts and regards wholesale theft, such as the inflation of the money supply, as a crime just as it does any other violation of contract.

From a legal point of view there is a way to protect the economy from fraudulent practices. Individuals or individuals collectively can seek clarity and justice by refining the definitions of property rights and then by insisting that they are protected.

Inherently and in accordance with the laws of human action, the divine economy allows the diverse expression that comes from individuals exercising their free will non-violently; and it also satisfies human needs, and it leads to an ever-advancing prosperity.

Selected Exercises

1. Imagine equilibrium acting like a pendulum, always bringing external forces back to the center.

   a. In your first diagram put 'consumer sovereignty' at the center position and imagine the forces that would cause movement away from consumer sovereignty. Describe these forces.

   b. In your second diagram put 'contracts' at the center position and describe the forces that move the economy away from contracts.

   c. Use the terminology of the divine economy theory to describe this tendency towards equilibrium.

2. Describe how the tendency of equilibrium is always present and yet at the same time the economy can still be ever-advancing.

Chapter 5
Economic Policy

The Fruits of the Divine Economy Model©

PREFACE

For all things there is a purpose and the purpose of the leaves and the branches and the purpose within, of creating a healthy microenvironment, is to yield fruit. This culmination once attained, and indicating maturity, continues over time and brings about prosperity. What we need to realize is that the fruit can be made more plentiful and more delicious when the system is balanced and wholesome.

HARVEST TIME

How do we get from the history of economic thought to useful steps for improving the economy? How can a model which is built upon recognition of the spiritual nature of man be of value in the real world? What good is it to tie economic principles to the modus operandi of the divine economy if there are no practical fruits? This is where policy comes in. It is a bridge between the theory and the application.

There are two things that I tried to clearly present about the divine economy. One is that it is powerful and transcendent, yet ever-present and nurturing. The other point of clarity is that the divine economy can be put into a corrupted or diseased condition by human intervention. The divine economy can never be destroyed, as evidenced by its equilibrating forces, but knowledge can be stifled and signals can be distorted by ego-driven intervention into the market process.

Knowing that the full potential of the divine economy can only be reached when intervention ceases may lead one to think that there should be no intervening policy. Contrarily, knowing that the justice that is inherent in the divine economy can only be reached if the market is free may lead one to think that there are policy steps to take to protect the divine economy from intervention, for the benefit of all mankind.

POLICY #1.
WELL DEFINED AND CONTINUALLY REFINED PROPERTY RIGHTS

It is clear that everything rests on property rights, which are mirror images of human rights. Not a single thing can happen that honors a person's human rights without acknowledging that these are also his or her property rights. Once this most basic right, the human right/property right, is defined the market process begins. As the property rights are refined the divine economy will empower human civilization to advance. See Diagram 5a. Without secure private property there will be little savings and investment and therefore little prosperity.

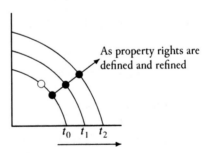

As property rights are defined and refined

An ever-advancing civilization

Diagram 5a: Production possibilities frontiers of well defined and continually refined property rights

What is the seed of property/human rights? The significant clue comes from Immanuel Kant: "Freedom ... is the only original right belonging to every man by virtue of his humanity."[4] When put into the context of the divine economy theory the uniqueness of each individual finds expression subjectively in one's choices, free choices that end up manifesting the characteristics of property in some form. As property rights are defined and refined the divine economy moves from t_0 to t_1 in Diagram 5b.

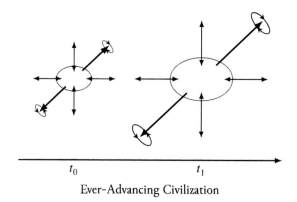

Ever-Advancing Civilization

Diagram 5b: Well defined and continually refined property rights advance the divine economy

POLICY STATEMENT: A rational and just policy would be to develop discovered laws that specifically define, refine, and protect property rights in terms such that they are treated and considered as basic human rights.

POLICY #2.
THE RIGHT OF SECESSION

At the social level the corollary of freedom implied in individual property rights is the right of secession. For a jurisdiction to guarantee its prosperity it will have to be able to protect property rights which may mean removing itself from the yoke of the oppressor, moving from t_0 to t_1 as shown in Diagram 5c.

It is time to bring back into common use a term that is understood in the classical liberalism tradition. That word is subsidiarity. It is the necessary complement to federation. Without subsidiarity even the logic of federation is thwarted, thus becoming potentially tyrannical. The guarantee of the maintenance of the balance brought about by the complements of subsidiarity and federation is the right of secession.

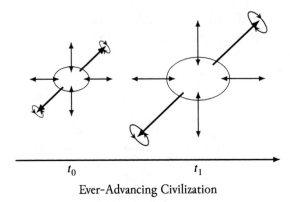

Ever-Advancing Civilization

Diagram 5c: Benefits from decentralization

Policies that release individual creativity by protecting liberty increase the awareness of knowledge and the awareness of how this knowledge activates in others the desire to know. As the realization of the rights to secede is internalized people will act with more confidence, and creativity will increase. This can be seen in Diagram 5d as the divine economy moves from t_0 to t_1 and beyond. Starting with the visualization of the complex divine economy model in mind we will then go to a shorthand version of the divine economy over time. The shorthand version focuses on the Justice/Unity axis which emphasizes the nature and role of knowledge in human civilization. See Diagram 5d.

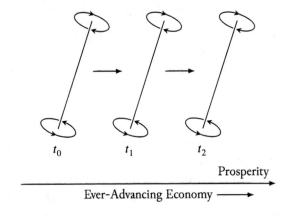

Prosperity

Ever-Advancing Economy ⟶

Diagram 5d: The right of secession advances the divine economy

POLICY STATEMENT: A rational policy would be to develop discovered law in such a way that a jurisdiction would not have to accept any intervention that a larger jurisdiction tried to impose upon its economy.

POLICY #3.
MARKET FORCES WILL MODERATE BUSINESS SIZES

In a market free from intervention firms can naturally become only so large. The inefficiencies of bureaucracy limit their sizes. For example, if a firm is vertically integrated—originally expanded in this manner to capture efficiency—but it becomes excessively large, then it begins to lose the ability to rationally allocate resources. Wages and factor prices in the internal (in-house) market begin to have no connection to the real market, become distorted and unrealistic, preventing the firm from being able to calculate. Smaller firms without these errors will begin to out-compete these overly bureaucratic firms.

When interventionist laws protect certain types of business ownerships by limiting the liability of the owners, it artificially encourages these firms to become very large since they are protected from the costs associated with damages to the property rights of independent third parties. In other words they are too large an entity to fight a legal battle against, plus finding out who exactly is responsible is very, very difficult. Therefore, limited liability for corporations causes distortions. Protection of property rights will ultimately make the economy serve the whole of mankind with justice rather than favoring institutions that are created by vested interests and which use intervention in an attempt to circumvent the forces of equilibrium. See Diagram 5e.

POLICY STATEMENT: A rational and just policy would be to remove the institutionalized barriers that prevent property rights from being protected, and to remove the special privileges that artificially protect any entity from the equilibrating forces of the divine economy.

POLICY #4.
ENFORCEMENT OF PROPERTY RIGHTS

The main policy recommendation derived from the divine economy model is to continually refine the definition of property rights. The corollary to this is to strengthen the legal system such that it can enforce property rights.

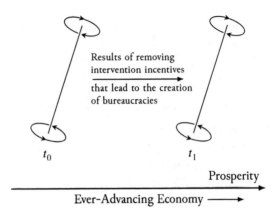

Diagram 5e: Allowing market forces to moderate business sizes advances the divine economy

The best means to protect private property rights is to strengthen the role of private enforcement providers since there is often a conflict of interest when the State is involved in protecting private property rights.

Both the definition of property rights and the ability to enforce property rights are currently weak, even weaker than they were 100 years ago. Needless to say the direction of that trend is wrongly oriented, away from progress, and needs to be set aright. See Diagram 5f.

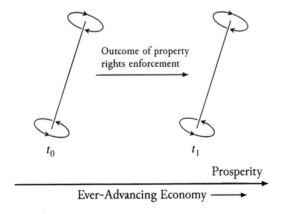

Diagram 5f: Enforcement of property rights advances the divine economy

POLICY STATEMENT: A rational policy would be to initially begin enforcing property rights at the level of the individual, and then to learn how best to refine property rights from these efforts. Within each community this right and responsibility exists and needs to be given due attention. The proper role of government is to protect its citizens from fraud or acts of violence by enforcing property rights, however, competition by private providers of legal protection will ensure that the best means of enforcing property rights is always available.

POLICY #5.
EDUCATION ABOUT ENTREPRENEURSHIP

Another policy that surfaces from looking at the divine economy model is to educate people about latent and active entrepreneurship. The purpose of educating people about entrepreneurship is basically to encourage and foster the acquisition of the skill of discernment. This comes from learning about the learning process in humans. The more discernment and alertness there is in the market the more quickly knowledge will flow and the more quickly will it be acted upon. This leads to an advancement of the market process and to prosperity. If the market is in an inefficient condition the solution is to educate people about entrepreneurship not to corrupt the divine economy by imposing arbitrary restrictions through intervention. See Diagram 5g.

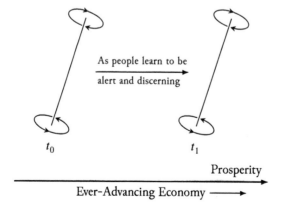

As people learn to be alert and discerning

t_0 t_1

Prosperity

Ever-Advancing Economy ⟶

Diagram 5g: Education about entrepreneurship advances the divine economy

POLICY STATEMENT: A rational policy would be to encourage all providers of education to acknowledge the role of entrepreneurship in advancing prosperity and to teach any and all skills that help to make people discerning and alert.

POLICY #6.
WAR AND INFLATION VIOLATE PROPERTY RIGHTS

Another policy that emerges from the divine economy model places emphasis again on education. It is clear from the concepts in the divine economy model that if people can trust the future they will have lower time preferences which will amplify the transforming capability of capital.

There are very specific interventions into the economy that strongly influence the level of trust. If there is a tendency to choose war as the main or even as a viable alternative to diplomacy then the lessened trust that such an act engenders atrophies the economy. Or if there is a medium of exchange that can easily be debased by a central bank (for example, when there is a fiat currency) then the horizon of the time preference shortens, stifling prosperity. Both of these acts of intervention—war and inflation by the central bank—violate the property rights of humanity. See Diagram 5h.

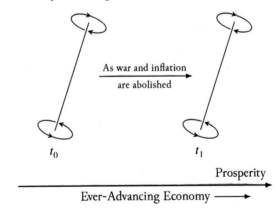

Diagram 5h: Abolishing war and inflation advances the divine economy

Those things that foster trust and trustworthiness need to be given particular emphasis as part of the learning process in the education system. The pivotal nature of property rights needs to be made crystal clear.

POLICY STATEMENT: War and its exorbitant costs and the associated destructiveness, and inflation of the money supply by the central bank, are unacceptable violations of property rights and those who try to impose either of these should be held accountable by legal means. Authority to take these actions needs to be specifically assigned so that there is specific and definite accountability.

The legal liability for such acts needs to take precedence over the act itself. The government-created veils of self-protection and inculpability need to be removed so that property rights can be protected.

POLICY #7.
GOLD PASSES THE MARKET TEST

Inflation reduces the purchasing power of money: and it causes the redistribution of wealth towards the ones favored by the interventionists. Both of these represent theft of private property and both are acts of injustice. The free market chose gold as the medium of exchange simply because of the following: it optimizes the characteristics determined in the market to be necessary for a trustworthy medium of exchange. The ability to strongly prevent dishonest and untrustworthy acts by the interventionists is certainly one of those characteristics and is a good reason to return to the gold standard.

Free banking, where banks compete against each other for the trust of their customers, is almost completely sufficient to safeguard against fraudulent banking practices. Combined with refined and enforced property rights it is wholly sufficient. Having a strong and honest banking system has the advantage of encouraging savings.

Free banking is a very important component of a divine economy since it has the merits of self-regulation, and since it serves the people by providing a storehouse for capital. This is in contrast to the current banking practices which mask the insolvencies of banks and promulgate a system of capital consumption and wealth redistribution. See Diagram 5i.

POLICY STATEMENT: Clear the banking system of all of its barriers and restrictions—these are acts of intervention designed to control the

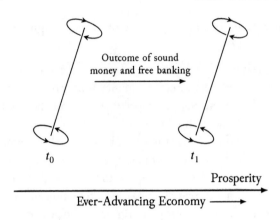

Diagram 5i: The gold standard advances the divine economy

economy and direct wealth towards the favored ones of the ego-driven interventionists—and let the market process determine if the current system is a viable one or not. Legal tender laws are unnecessary in a divine economy where the medium of exchange is universally recognized simply because of its independence from monetary intervention along with its other merits.

POLICY #8.
COUNTERACT THE MISINFORMATION ABOUT CAPITAL

There is a very difficult educational task ahead to counteract the institutionalized prejudice against capitalism. Capital has been maligned and misunderstood for so long that most people feel that capital is not really a part of themselves—that it is outside of themselves. One goal of the educator will be to help people to see that every choice or act to improve oneself is capital in process and capital made manifest. And the improvement made is then an advancement and the starting point for the next step.

Appreciation of capital, when seen as honoring one's own progress, will go a long way towards reversing the poisonous bigotry directed at capital which permeates the world today. The anti-capitalist mentality is a malady emanating from Marxism, socialism and much of empirical economics. It stems from a combination of atheism and the adherence to an incorrect methodology for the social sciences, and it leads to a removal of capital from its proper place in the human psyche. Our inherent nature declares capital to be a vital part of the human operating system—and the divine economy itself, which is entrusted to us, shuns such an ill-fated attempt. See Diagram 5j.

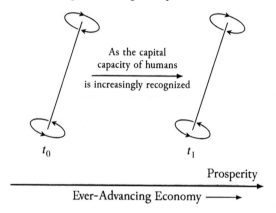

As the capital capacity of humans is increasingly recognized

t_0 t_1

Prosperity

Ever-Advancing Economy ⟶

Diagram 5j: Understanding capital advances the divine economy

POLICY STATEMENT: Encourage providers of education to recognize that every improvement an individual makes—their education, for example— is a form of capital. Then instead of spreading negative impressions about capital the education system will compliment itself for being a contributor to capital formation around the world and will empower the next generation with knowledge about this factor—capital. This is a significant contribution to an ever-advancing civilization since capital is the most limiting factor in the economy.

POLICY #9.
NEW CAPITAL IS A GOOD START

Assuming that some of those who use this book will be concerned about an economy that is undeveloped (although this principle operates in more advanced economies as well), the first steps taken should be to encourage and nurture capital. Unprotected property rights are very often the reason people do not save. Any steps that secure property rights and foster trustworthiness lead to the emergence of new capital. New capital advances productivity and then the development process begins. See Diagram 5k.

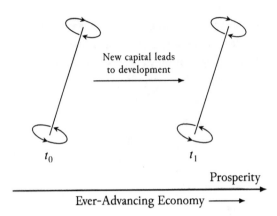

New capital leads
to development

t_0 t_1

Prosperity

Ever-Advancing Economy ———▶

Diagram 5k: New capital advances the divine economy

POLICY STATEMENT: Recognize that having secure property rights leads to savings and then to new capital which then begins the advancement towards prosperity.

POLICY #10.
INTERNATIONAL FREE TRADE

Another self-evident policy recommendation is to recognize that the divine economy works at all times and it works regardless of scale. The same benefits that come to an individual when taking part in exchange in the market occur with trade at the international level. Only international free trade allows the prosperity of the divine economy to be fully released. Artificial and imaginary boundary restrictions are simply interventions that lessen the prosperity that can come from the divine economy and these interventions do damage to the advancement of civilization. Only international division of labor under a system of secure property rights and free trade brings the resources of the world to the market efficiently and with justice—for all to enjoy. See Diagram 5l.

POLICY STATEMENT: All trade barriers interfere with the divine economy and cause unnecessary suffering. 'Free trade' agreements are really acts of intervention and therefore are a misnomer. Free trade, in reality, is action not words and it will occur automatically if the ego-driven interventionists are removed from the picture.

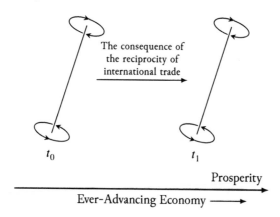

Diagram 5l: International free trade advances the divine economy

POLICY #11.
MINIMAL TAXATION

If you go back and look at the Divine Economy Model © you will notice that taxation does not appear to be present at all in the model. What this means is that, theoretically speaking, taxation is not necessarily present in a divine economy. Taxation is not necessarily absent either.

Economics is the study of the means to obtain the ends chosen. If some type of taxation is the best means for achieving order in a cooperative society that protects life and liberty then taxation serves a purpose and it is present. See Diagram 5m.

In a society where property rights are well-defined, and refined, and protected, taxation will be either minimal or absent. As long as taxation is restrained by laws that protect and enforce property rights then taxes will be held to a minimum. The law and order of the divine economy is a reflection of life and liberty which means that taxes need to be zero or minimal so as not to disrupt the flow of knowledge inherent in the free market process. See Diagrams 5n and 5o.

POLICY STATEMENT: Since under most circumstances taxation is a deterrent to private production and employment there is no sound economic reason to generate tax revenue to support a government beyond its purpose. The purpose of government is to protect life and liberty.

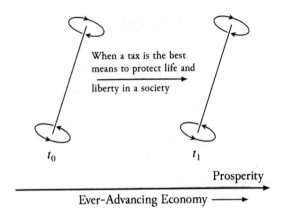

When a tax is the best means to protect life and liberty in a society

t_0

t_1

Prosperity

Ever-Advancing Economy

Diagram 5m: Minimal taxation advances the divine economy

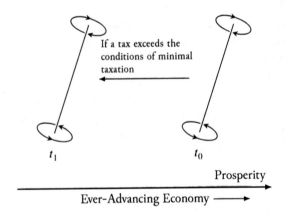

If a tax exceeds the conditions of minimal taxation

t_1

t_0

Prosperity

Ever-Advancing Economy

Diagram 5n: Contracting economy caused by taxation

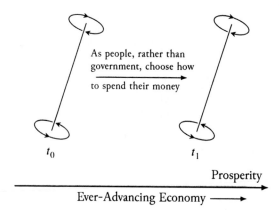

As people, rather than
government, choose how

to spend their money

t_0 t_1

Prosperity

Ever-Advancing Economy ⟶

Diagram 5o: When the economy reflects the people the divine economy advances

The Overarching Policy —
The Moral Authority of the Divine Economy

To quote Ludwig von Mises: "The first condition for the establishment of perpetual peace is the general adoption of the principles of laissez-faire capitalism."[9, p. 137]

I would like to modify his recommendation slightly. First, we can rest assured that the prosperity of an ever-advancing civilization emanates from the divine economy. Second, we can trust in the equilibrating power of the divine economy. Third, we can trust in the divine justice that comes from protecting property rights and that comes from recognizing that property rights are human rights.

Those who fail to admit their own limitations and then expect others to believe their assertions that they can comprehend all that is going on in the economy — thereby giving them the right to interfere — these are the ones who are now without authority. It matters not what position of influence one holds or what degree one has or what record of publication one has. There is no human act of intervention in the economy that is not feeble-minded when compared with the omnipotent and omnipresent nature of God.

All interference with the economy is necessarily ego-driven; and it lacks moral authority. The economy is a divine institution in the domain of human action and all human action emanates from the human operating system, which is divine — created in the image of God.

Using the concepts and graphics of the Divine Economy Model ©
we can focus our attention on policies that lead to an ever-advancing
civilization. But first we have to understand the moral authority of the
divine economy. As humans perfect themselves physically, intellectually and spiritually the divine economy expands and matures (moving
from t_0 to t_1) as shown in Diagram 5p. Policies that support and sustain
liberty and property rights as human rights allow the divine economy
to move towards fruition.

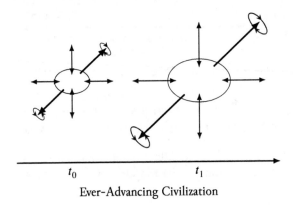

Ever-Advancing Civilization

Diagram 5p: The divine economy expands

The driving force of the economy is entrepreneurship. It is the
entrepreneurial spirit within humans that discovers betterment. See
Diagram 5q.

Policies that convert latent entrepreneurship into active entrepreneurship and policies that encourage alertness and discernment expand
the overall potential of entrepreneurship in the minds of all. When
market information is free from the distortion caused by intervention
the divine economy is in a charged state releasing an increased power of
human creativity as shown in Diagram 5q. Policies that are conducive
to building a link between capital and entrepreneurship complete the
transformation implied and described by the recurring designation
'Ever-Advancing Civilization.'

One thing is for sure and that is that the economy is dynamic, not
static. It is always somewhere along a dynamic spectrum (Diagram 5r),
either regressive or progressive.

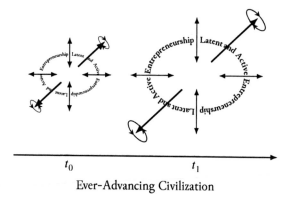

Ever-Advancing Civilization

Diagram 5q: Expanding entrepreneurship in the divine economy

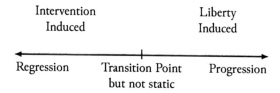

Intervention	Liberty
Induced	Induced

Regression Transition Point Progression
     but not static

Diagram 5r: Dynamic spectrum of the divine economy

Policies that foster the nature and role of knowledge in the individual and in the market carry forward an ever-advancing civilization. Implied in the 'nature of knowledge' is the refinement and progress of human learning. And implied in the 'role of knowledge' is economic communication by the means of market prices and voluntary worldwide trade.

Policies that promote justice and unity (Diagram 5s) universally stem from the preservation of both the nature and the role of knowledge; that is, preservation and protection from those who have ego-driven motives. It is the ego-driven who try to interfere with the nature of knowledge since they are the ones who benefit from the existence of prejudices, superstitions, and ignorance. Likewise it is the ego-driven who try to manipulate the economy through intervention, all for the purpose of benefiting themselves directly or indirectly.

Each of these eleven simple policies given in this chapter fall within the overarching policy of the moral authority of the divine economy and

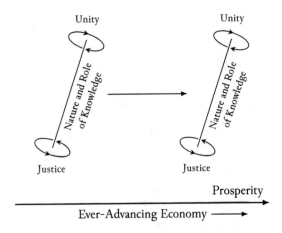

Diagram 5s: Divine economy and the ever-advancing civilization

will effectively promote an ever-advancing civilization in various ways. All of them also compliment each other. Of keen interest is the fact that all of these policies represent positive changes that have been brought to the forefront of our attention by the divine economy theory.

Selected Exercises

1. Which of these eleven policies do you understand the most? The least?

2. Why is the right of secession supportive of human rights and minimal taxation?

3. Compare and contrast the moral authority of laissez-faire economics with the moral authority of the divine economy theory.

Epilogue: Economic Transition

The Seeds of the Divine Economy Model©

PREFACE

Once the luscious fruit is discovered and its source and foundation is nurtured the time comes for its propagation. The advantage of propagating by seed is the ease of its ability to be distributed. It is something that starts small and it permits the steward to become more knowledgeable over time. It comes with a guarantee: if it is planted in the soil of inviolate private property rights it will survive and flourish and bring great prosperity.

PLANTING THE SEED

The divine economy model introduced in Chapter 2 is a gem and a germ. It is a powerful tool for bringing economic principles into the light for further examination.

From this point forward I propose to you that the science of economics, which is often referred to as the 'dismal science,' is instead seen as a bright and hopeful study of purposeful human action!

I have written this book to uncover what seemed to be hidden and to connect it to the vast economic knowledge that emerged from the tradition of classical liberalism. My goal with this book is to make clear much of the mystery about how the economy works and to also make it clear that there is no justification for human interference.

I have played a useful role by creating, in this work, a palatable and moral economics model as suggested by Ludwig von Mises:

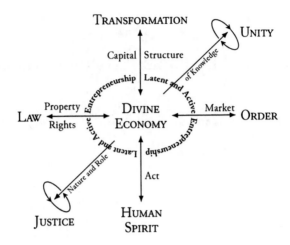

The flowering of human society depends on two factors: the intellectual power of outstanding men to conceive sound social and economic theories, and the ability of these or other men to make these ideologies palatable to the majority. [11, p. 985]

During the current period of economic transition that we live in, this book and other contributions to the divine economy theory[1,2,3] are the seeds waiting to be planted in the fertile minds of the economists of the future. These seeds will germinate once they are watered with the pure water of subjectivism and fertilized with an ardent search for an understanding of divine reality.

1. *HUMAN ESSENCE of Economics* (2009)
2. *ETHICAL ECONOMICS for today and tomorrow...* (2010)
3. *Liberty & Justice of Economic Equilibrium* (2011)

Glossary

Active Entrepreneurship: A state of alertness where opportunities are easily discerned to be acted upon.

Capital: The financial resources which are necessary for the production of most current goods and all future goods.

Disequilibrium: The real economic condition that exists in the world because of uncertainty and imperfect knowledge.

Disutility of Labor: Regarding the three qualities of the human reality—physical, intellectual, and spiritual—humans least prefer the strenuous pathways.

Divine Economy: The equilibrium force that is at the center of the divine institution—the economy—that has been bestowed upon humankind by God.

Divine Economy Model: A subjectivist model that describes the economy in the following terms: human spirit, transformation, law, order, purposeful action, capital structure, market, property rights, justice, and unity.

Divine Economy Theory: The theory that uses the subjectivist methodology to explore how the human identity of being created in the 'image of God' helps us to understand how the economy works.

Division of labor: Since every human being is unique, as they pursue their goals there is the potential that they will make a unique contribution to production.

Empiricism: The use of data rather than theory to explain things.

Equilibrium: The tendency towards balance and harmony.

Ever-advancing civilization: Humans, individually and as a whole, always aspire towards and potentially achieve greater perfections.

Hampered Economy: This is an economy where acts of intervention interfere with the equilibrium forces.

Human Operating System: All of the inherent human faculties that serve as the means to fulfill our human purpose, which ultimately is to know and love God.

Inflation: Artificial expansion of the money supply.

Intervention: Imposition of finite human acts of control onto an infinite and divine system.

Laissez-faire: An economic philosophy based on the insight that the economy works best when there is no intervention.

Latent Entrepreneurship: A state of potential unachieved due to discernment dormancy.

Leisure: The desire to satisfy one's highest valued physical, intellectual, or spiritual aspiration instead of working.

Macroeconomy: A term used to indicate that aggregate indicators in the economy are being looked at.

Market: The place and process where information flows between and among participants.

Market Process: A natural and universal process that functions like a language does to facilitate the making of exchanges.

Production Possibilities Frontier: A macroeconomic tool using two opposing aggregates to explain the limits of production.

Purchasing Power: A measure of the value of the medium of exchange in terms of the goods that can be purchased per unit of money.

Savings: The portion of income set aside for future consumption.

Secession: The right to leave a jurisdictional arrangement in a contractual society.

Standard of Living: An aggregate reference point assessing the degree of well-being and prosperity in relative terms.

Subjectivism: The scientific approach that recognizes that humans act subjectively, and this then leads to realistic and relevant scientific discoveries.

Taxation: Coercive extraction of wealth by government.

Time Preference: The universal law of human action that states that people prefer to have a good now rather than that same good sometime in the future.

Unhampered Economy: A synonym for a laissez-faire economy and a free market economy. It is also the condition that exists in a divine economy.

List of References

[1] Bartolome de Albornoz. *Arte de los Contratos.* Valencia, 1573.

[2] Roger Garrison. *Time and Money: The Macroeconomics of Capital Structure.* Routledge, London and New York, 2001.

[3] F. A. Hayek. The use of knowledge in society. *The American Economic Review,* XXXV(4), September 1945.

[4] Immanuel Kant. *The Metaphysics of Morals.* Cambridge University Press, 1996. tr. by Mary Gregor, with an intro. by Roger Sullivan.

[5] Israel M. Kirzner. *Competition & Entrepreneurship.* University of Chicago Press, Chicago, 1973.

[6] George Reisman. Classical economics vs. the exploitation theory. In Kurt R. Leube and Albert H. Zlabinger, editors, *The Political Economy of Freedom: Essays in Honor of F. A. Hayek.* Philosophia Verlag, The International Carl Menger Library, München and Wien, 1985.

[7] Murray N. Rothbard. *The Ethics of Liberty.* New York University Press, New York, 1998.

[8] Murray N. Rothbard. *Man, Economy, and State.* Ludwig von Mises Institute, scholar's edition, 2004.

[9] Ludwig von Mises. *The Ultimate Foundation of Economic Science.* Sheed Andrews & McMeel, Kansas City, 1978.

[10] Ludwig von Mises. *Theory and History.* The Ludwig von Mises Institute, 1985.

[11] Ludwig von Mises. *Human Action.* Fox & Wilkes, San Francisco, fourth revised edition, 1996.

Index

About the Author

Bruce Koerber—the originator of the divine economy theory and the divine economy models.

The whole theory and the associated models developed as part of a deductive process. The simple model appeared to be organic and easily took on the characteristics inherent in the philosophy of classical liberalism. The first stage of its development ended with a dynamic macroeconomic model. Pursuing further the deductive process the model fit perfectly into a structural analysis that penetrated into the very heart of economic activity all the way to the origin of where value comes from. This discovery process yielded the microeconomic model.

Two major realms of the divine economy model remained unexplored. The first was the ethical strand which had to do with the connection between the human spirit expressed as purposeful human action, and transformation which is manifest in the capital structure. The perspective of the divine economy theory renewed macro and micro economics, granted, but the melding together of ethics and economics in theory and in a model had never been achieved before.

The last component of the divine economy model is just as earthshaking. This time the relationship between law and order brought to light the role of the equilibrium forces of the economy in the advancement of civilization by balancing all aspects of social cooperation, most notably liberty and justice.